VERTICAL LIVING

Aligning Your Heart With God's Will

DEBORAH ELLINGTON WHITE

What Others Are Saying

The invitation to prayer can be found throughout the Bible from Genesis to Revelation. In Vertical Living, author DeBorah White broadens the reader's perspective on prayer by presenting an engaging, thought-provoking discourse on the necessity and value of prayer.

While numerous books have been written on the subject of prayer, prayer remains a topic ripe for even deeper exploration. Greater insight is needed to fully capitalize and understand this rich opportunity that has been presented to believers and unbelievers, alike. How should we pray? When should we pray? How do we press beyond our failures? Vertical Living addresses these practical questions and steers the reader towards the Biblical principles that will enhance their prayer life.

Throughout the book, DeBorah White shares her own personal experiences which include painstaking tragedies that helped her cultivate a greater appreciation for prayer. The deeply personal stories of triumph in the midst of tragedy aid in creating a relaxed reading environment. It is an environment that invites the reader to glean from the wisdom shared by the author, without wrestling with feelings of guilt or condemnation.

Vertical Living will provide a loving nudge and practical blue print for exploring and rediscovering the significance of prayer.

Dr. Yasha Jones-Becton, Author,
Appreciating the Value of Nothing

Awesome! As church leaders we sometimes focus on those horizontal things that can sometimes distract us (personnel issues, budgets, programs and policies) rather than looking up to God. After reading this I realize that we cannot do it all by ourselves but we really do need God's help to fix it. I am challenged to stop focusing on my horizontal communications with God, but rather on my vertical conversations with Him. DeBorah White's book Vertical Living has captured the essentials of our prayer life with God.

Pastor Randal "Mack" Jackson, Assistant Pastor, Bible Way Church Atlas Road

---

Inspiring, Profound, and Motivational!

God is speaking through DeBorah to all who will take the time to read this book with a hunger and desire to be fed, strengthened, informed, and encouraged. I love the challenges and the sharing. There is joy, there is inquiry, there is surprise and elation – countered with tears of awareness, sobriety, and gratefulness. From God's lips to DeBorah's keyboard…what a blessing!!!

Dr. Regina Shearer, Associate Vice President for Student Success, Rivier University

VERTICAL LIVING

VERTICAL LIVING by DeBorah Ellington White

This book or parts thereof may not be reproduced in any form, stored in a retrieval system, or transmitted in any form by any means—electronic, mechanical, photocopy, recording, or otherwise—without prior written permission of the publisher, except as provided by United States of America copyright law.

Scripture quotations marked AMP are from the Amplified Bible. Copyright © 1954, 1958, 1962, 1964, 1965, 1987 by The Lockman Foundation. Used by permission.

Scripture quotations marked AMPC are from the Amplified Bible, Classic Edition. Copyright © 1954, 1958, 1962, 1964, 1965, 1987 by The Lockman Foundation. Used by permission.

Scripture quotations marked ESV are from the Holy Bible, English Standard Version. Copyright © 2001 by Crossway Bibles, a division of Good News Publishers. Used by permission.

Scripture quotations marked GNT are taken from the Holy Bible, Good News Translation. Copyright © 1992 by God's Word to the Nations. Used by permission of Baker Publishing Group.

Scripture quotations marked GWT are taken from GOD'S WORD Translation. Copyright © 1995 by God's Word to the Nations. Used by permission of Baker Publishing Group.

Scripture quotations marked HCSB are taken from the Holman Christian Standard Bible®, Copyright © 1999, 2000, 2002, 2003, 2009 by Holman Bible Publishers. Used by permission. Holman Christian Standard Bible®, Holman CSB®, and HCSB® are federally registered trademarks of Holman Bible Publishers.

Scripture quotations marked KJV are from the King James Version of the Bible.

Scripture quotations marked NASB are from the New American Standard Bible, copyright © 1960, 1962, 1963, 1968, 1971, 1972, 1973, 1975, 1977, 1995 by The Lockman Foundation. Used by permission. (www.Lockman.org)

Scripture quotations marked NCV are taken from the New Century Version®. Copyright © 2005 by Thomas Nelson. Used by permission. All rights reserved.

Scripture quotations marked NET BIBLE are from the New English Translation. Copyright © 1996-2006 by Biblical Studies Press, L.L.C. http://netbible.com All rights reserved.

Scripture quotations marked NIV are taken from the Holy Bible, New International Version®, NIV®. Copyright © 1973, 1978, 1984, 2011 by Biblica, Inc.™ Used by permission of Zondervan. All rights reserved worldwide. www.zondervan.com The "NIV" and "New International Version" are trademarks registered in the United States Patent and Trademark Office by Biblica, Inc.™

Scripture quotations marked NKJV are taken from the New King James Version®. Copyright © 1982 by Thomas Nelson. Used by permission. All rights reserved.

Scripture quotations marked NLT are from the Holy Bible, New Living Translation, copyright © 1996, 2004, 2007. Used by permission of Tyndale House Publishers, Inc., Wheaton, IL 60189. All rights reserved.

Scripture quotations marked NLV are from the Holy Bible, New Life Version, copyright © 1969. Used by permission of Christian Literature International. All rights reserved.

Scripture quotations marked PHILLIPS are from The New Testament in Modern English, Revised Edition. Copyright © 1958, 1960, 1972 by J. B. Phillips. Macmillan Publishing Co. Used by permission.

Scripture quotations marked THE MESSAGE are from The Message: The Bible in Contemporary English, copyright © 1993, 1994, 1995, 1996, 2000, 2001, 2002. Used by permission of NavPress Publishing Group.

Scripture quotations marked TLB are from The Living Bible. Copyright © 1971. Used by permission of Tyndale House Publishers, Inc., Wheaton, IL 60189. All rights reserved.

Copyright © 2016 by DeBorah Ellington White

All rights reserved

Cover design by Say It Like This Designs, LLC

Visit the author's website at deborahewhite.com

Library of Congress Cataloging-in-Publication Data:

An application to register this book for cataloging has been submitted to the Library of Congress.

International Standard Book Number: 978-0- 9972921-2-1

E-book ISBN: 978-1- 945304-70-5

While the author has made every effort to provide accurate Internet addresses at the time of publication, neither the publisher nor the author assumes any responsibility for errors or for changes that occur after publication.

Dedication

In loving memory...

I am most grateful to my grandparents, the late Reverend Richard and Carrie Ravenel. Affectionately, my Dad and Mom. They introduced me to Christ, baptized me and, at a young age, instilled in me a strong foundation in prayer and godly-living. There was never a need to look further than our front door for a living—breathing— example of a godly man or woman. Though not present, their spirit and mantle are forever with me.

Contents

Dedication ix

1   *Vertical Living* 1
    Introduction 3

2   *Part I: Vertical Life* 7
    Chapter 1: An Open Invitation 9
    Chapter 2: A Confident Approach 13
    Chapter 3: Finding God's Frequency............................19
    Chapter 4: Exhaust Him 25
    Chapter 5: Can Prayer Really Change This? 31
    Chapter 6: Don't Play with Your Weakness 37
    Chapter 7: 24/7 43
    Chapter 8: What Could Be Better? 49

3   *Part II: Vertical Focus* 53
    Chapter 9: Vertical Focus 55
    Chapter 10: Distractions 57
    Chapter 11: Waterfalls 61
    Chapter 12: Hitting the Wall! 67

4	*Part III: Vertical View in Distress, Grief and Loss*	71
	Chapter 13: Life Hurts	73
	Chapter 14: Lord, Keep My Mind!	77
	Chapter 15: A Message for Your Womb	81
	Chapter 16: No Longer Sad	85
5	*Part IV: Vertical View in Perceived Failure*	95
	Chapter 17: More Than Able	97
	Chapter 18: I Can Fix It!	101
	Chapter 19: The Finished Product	105
6	*Part V: Vertical View in Chaos and Crisis*	111
	Chapter 20: I Know You Weren't Prepared for This!	113
	Chapter 21: Before You Go to Pieces	121
	Chapter 22: Hunker Down	123
7	*Part VI: Vertical Lifeline*	129
	Chapter 23: Pray First	131
	Appendix: Connect in Prayer	137
8	*Notes*	143

Vertical Living

We do this by keeping our eyes on Jesus, the champion who initiates and perfects our faith.

—Hebrews 12:2

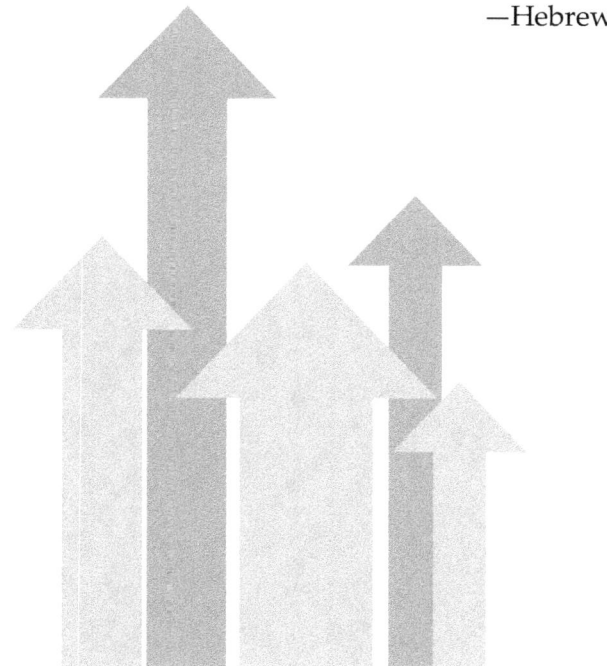

Introduction

[The enemy] will flatter those who hate the things of God and win them over to his side. But the people who know their God shall be strong and do great things.

—DANIEL 11:32, TLB

Evangelist and Bible teacher Oswald Chambers is quoted as saying, "Prayer does not fit us for the greater work; prayer is the greater work."[1] Every man or woman who ever has done or is doing something great for God has been a man or woman of prayer. They are who they are because they make prayer a priority in their lives. The more you pray, the richer your prayer life becomes. The richer your prayer life becomes, the closer your relationship is with the Father. The more intimate your relationship is with Him, the more God can trust you. And the more He can trust you, the stronger and more powerful you become in Him.

Vertical Living is a reminder of the great grace and benefits of access we have in our heavenly Father. It is a call to keep our focus and attention on God, and choose to have a godly perspective about everything we encounter. It is an encouragement to choose prayer over worry, anxiety, despair, and the world's horizontal ideologies of conflict resolution.

This book shares wisdom the Lord has given me over the years, which I pray is constructed in a way that will captivate your heart and move you toward successful biblical living through the power of prayer. Some of the chapters share my personal struggle in transforming from immaturity to being Spirit-led in all of my decision-making. In every chapter, I hope to encourage you to realize the power that lies within you. You may use this book as part of your daily devotion or as a tool for witnessing to those you meet along the way. Take time to study the Scripture verses within these pages to sharpen your knowledge of God's Word concerning His plan for your life. Pray them over your life, your family, your friends, and others.

In addition to Scripture verses, I have included encouraging quotes relating to each chapter's topic. And at the end of the book, in the Appendix, are examples of prayers to give you that vertical lift as you start to cultivate a lifetime practice of daily communion with the Father. It is my hope that you will apply what you read. After all, "Knowledge without application is like a book that is never read."[2]

As you read these pages, take time to think about how you plan to take advantage of your power and exercise your privilege. Reflect on how you can become more disciplined in your communication with God. When you pray, ask the Father to increase your capacity for prayer so you can improve your vertical reach.

It is my prayer that you will be encouraged while reading these pages and that the essentials of effective prayer will become as natural to you as breathing. I pray that you will embrace the vastness of God's love and the depth of His grace toward you. Finally, I pray that these words will inspire you to grab the horns of the altar of prayer and never let go, no matter what obstacles you face in this life.

Won't you go to the Father today?

> *When I think of all this, I fall to my knees and pray to the Father, the Creator of everything in heaven and on earth. I pray that from his glorious, unlimited resources he will empower you with inner strength through his Spirit. Then Christ will make his home in your hearts as you trust in him. Your roots will grow down into God's love and keep you strong. And may you have the power to understand, as all God's people should, how wide, how long, how high, and how deep his love is. May you experience the love of Christ, though it is too great to understand fully. Then you will be made complete with all the fullness of life and power that comes from God.*
>
> —Ephesian 5:14-19

Part I
Vertical Life

Lift Up Your Eyes and See.

—Psalm 121:1

Chapter 1
An Open Invitation

Prayer is God's invitation to enter His throne room so He can lay His agenda over our hearts.

—HENRY T. BLACKABY

Prayer is the greatest invitation we will receive from the Father.

An invitation is a written or spoken request for someone to go somewhere or do something. From what I recall about etiquette, when you receive an invitation, particularly one including an RSVP (please reply), you are supposed to respond in a timely manner and then show up at the specified time. There is nothing worse than inviting someone to your home and having them accept the invitation, and then after you've prepared for their arrival, they not only don't show, but they don't even let you know they aren't coming.

An open-ended invitation, however, is different. It is very hard to decline because there is no pressure for you to give a definitive answer about whether you will attend. Any time you are available to show up is the perfect time for you to arrive.

That is the kind of invitation the Father is extending to us. Prayer is a very personal invitation from the Father, and the RSVP is open-ended. The Father is saying, "No pressure." We are welcome to meet with Him any time we feel the need to visit. And since the invitation is open-ended, "I'm too busy" is going to be a hard excuse to sell.

As my husband often reminds our congregation "How can the recipient of time tell the giver of time we don't have time?" The Father wants us to know that prayer does not happen when He shows up. Prayer happens when we show up.

We may not readily respond to the Father's invitation to meet with Him in prayer because we are afraid to bring our requests to God or talk to Him about our deepest desires. Perhaps we feel ashamed of our failures and unworthy to come before Him. Or maybe we severely undervalue our importance in the Father's eyes.

But when the Father invites us to come to Him in prayer, He already knows who and what we are. He created us. Moreover, there is nothing about us that shocks Him. The more we actively come before Him, the more we change into the image of His Son—"For those God foreknew he also predestined to be conformed to the image of his Son" (Rom. 8:29, NIV).

As you develop a daily habit of spending time in God's presence, try letting go of what your natural eyes see and what you think of yourself. Begin to see yourself as God sees you. You will soon discover there will be days when you cannot wait to spend time with Him.

Prayer can be intimidating whether you have known God for a long time or you have just received Christ as your Lord and Savior. How is a person supposed to pray? Do we use a prayer book and recite a series of written prayers? Do we have to follow a particular structure or model? What is the right way to pray?

Prayer does not need to be a complicated thing. It does not need to be long or drawn out. It does not need to be loud, memorized, or formal. We do not have to know all the right words to say in order to come before the Lord. God wants to hear our heart, not just our words.

The awesome thing about God is that He desires to be a part of every intimate detail of our lives. He wants us to simply talk to Him as our Father, in prayers of petition (praying for ourselves) or prayers of intercession (praying for others), to believe by faith that He will come through for us, and then to thank Him for the answer in advance. However, in order for prayer to become a regular part of our lives, it needs to become something we look forward to doing.

James 1:25 tells us how important a daily time with God is.

> *But the man who looks into the perfect mirror of God's law, the law of liberty (or freedom), and makes a habit of so doing, is not the man who sees and forgets. He puts that law into practice and he wins true happiness.*
>
> —PHILLIPS

Some people call it devotion, some meditation, but prayer is simply spending time with God. As we set aside time to be alone with the Father each day, we get to know Him both through prayer and by studying His Word.

When we give God our time, we open the door for the Holy Spirit to speak to us through His Word. As we hear and read the Word daily, we prepare our spirit to hear directly from God. In other words, when we develop a daily habit of spending time with God and studying His Word, the Holy Spirit is able to bring that Word back to our remembrance during times of tests and trials. In addition, knowing God's Word gives us greater discernment, and we become able to declare specific scriptures in prayer and take authority over our day. The benefits of accepting God's invitation to prayer are endless.

Chapter 2
A Confident Approach

Therefore, let us draw near with confidence to the throne of grace, so that we may receive mercy and find grace to help in time of need.

—HEBREWS 4:6, NIV

How we approach God in prayer is just as important as the physical posture we take. We know we can kneel, stand, lie prostrate, etc., in prayer, but posture is as much about attitude as it is about a physical stance. The posture we should have in prayer is one of confidence.

Most people confuse having confidence with arrogance. However, they are two distinctly different things. Arrogance is "an insulting way of thinking or behaving that comes from believing that you are better, smarter, or more important than other people."[1] Arrogance is about the intent of our hearts. It is when ability or perceived ability can be used to look down on others.

Confidence, on the other hand, is the unshakable belief in the power, trustworthiness, or reliability of a person or thing greater than one's self.[2] It is the feeling or belief that one can rely on someone or something, having a firm trust. It also means we are invited to express ourselves freely, with an openness or boldness, even in the midst of obvious intimidation.

In prayer, we can have confidence in what God says about His character and believe He has the power to bring to pass the things He promised. Moreover, Luke 1:37 tells us His word never fails. Therefore, we can follow God, having full confidence in His wisdom, power, and plan.

Confidence should do three things in the life of a believer as it pertains to prayer.

Confidence Ignites Faith

> *And without faith it is impossible to please Him for he who comes to God must believe that He is and that He is a rewarder of those who seek Him.*
>
> —HEBREWS 11:6, NASB

The text implies that we must have faith mixed with confidence when we look to God. The words faith, trust, and belief all come from one Greek root word, pístis, which means to persuade or to be persuaded.[3] All three words indicate a transfer of our trust from our ability to God's ability. We trust in what He has promised. We trust in what He has done and will do.

Because His Word does not fail, it makes sense that we should have an unshakeable belief in the power of God—the power to save us, the power to heal us, and, yes, the power to make us free. We should have an unshakeable belief in God's trustworthiness. We can trust Him, Jeremiah says, because He is faithful (Jer. 1:12). In Lamentations 3, we read that confidence is a hopefulness that events will be favorable. Even when we are not faithful, our Father has a duty to perform. The apostle Paul told Timothy "If we are faithless, He remains faithful, for He cannot deny Himself" (2 Tim. 2:13, NASB).

Confidence Brings Order to Chaos

When our life is full of chaos and we are unable to trust our own emotions, thoughts, or decisions, we can trust God. We should have an unshakable confidence that God will always be there for us. The prophet Isaiah says you can rely on Him!

> *When you pass through the waters, I will be with you.*
>
> —ISAIAH 43:2, NASB, EMPHASIS ADDED

What is required for us to live through the chaos, when things begin to change and life is not what we planned or envisioned it would be? Isaiah says we can rely on God whether there is order or chaos. Even in the midst of a changing culture, we can stay calm. With this confidence, we can respond instead of reacting to the things around us. When we have confidence in God, we cannot be manipulated by the philosophy of our world.

Daniel chapter 3 tells the story of three Hebrew teenagers—Shadrach, Meshach, and Abednego—who were challenged to make a decision to follow God in the midst of a chaotic culture. King Nebuchadnezzar decreed that everyone must bow before an image of himself that he had erected. Can you imagine what it must have looked like for thousands of people to kneel before a statute of the king? But when everyone else was kneeling, these three young men chose to stand. And everybody knew this was the posture they took.

When we read the story in God's Word, we are told of their courage. But I am not sure they were truly courageous; I believe they had great confidence in their God. Confidence will give way to courage. Confidence inspired the apostle Paul to write in Ephesians 3:12, "In him [Christ] and through faith in him we may approach God with freedom and confidence" (NIV). This confidence gives us the ability to succeed in life.

Confidence Creates Reward

The apostle Paul approached God with freedom and confidence. Then in Hebrews 10:35, he admonished us not to cast away, discard, or give up our confidence in Him merely because the world does not understand—because if we do, we could be throwing away the rich (abundant) reward attached to it. God is faithful and He honors our confidence in Him. It is important that we know where our confidence lies. It is not in our flesh; it is not in our own ability or the ability of others. Our confidence is in Christ Jesus. And He is our example of confidence.

Confidence is of God. If you do not have it, it is not because God does not want you to have it. It is because you have chosen not to believe about yourself what God would have you to believe. A confident person feels competent from the inside out, because he or she has the greater one operating on the inside. When Jesus declared that God hears Him when He prays (John 11:42), He embodied a confidence in the Father that was completely unshakable.

In his first epistle, John wrote "This is the confidence we have in approaching God: that if we ask anything according to his will, he hears us" (1 John 5:14, NIV, emphasis added). This same confidence has passed to every believer. If anyone in the world is going to be overly confident, it should be the believer. And our "overconfidence" should be in God.

The Father invites you and me to come up higher, to a vertical fellowship, and embrace His love and His agenda. If you accept, that acceptance must be real and authentic, and you must have confidence that the God you serve is all-knowing, all-powerful, and fully able to do exceedingly abundantly above all that you could ask or think.

Chapter 3
Finding God's Frequency

God is a frequency. Stay tuned.

—ALAN COHEN

Whenever I have an opportunity to travel long distances, my preferred mode of transportation is by airplane. That is simply because, much like little children, I find it really challenging to ride in a car longer than three hours.

While most people use their time in the air reading or playing computer games, I find flying allows me to catch up on some much-needed sleep. However, for some reason, I cannot relax enough to close my eyes until after the flight attendants have given the cabin instructions and pointed out the safety features of the aircraft. Before I fall asleep, the last thing I usually hear is, "Should the plane lose power, the cabin is equipped with lighting along the floors. Should there be a sudden change in cabin pressure an oxygen mask will drop from overhead. If you are travelling with a small child, be sure to place the oxygen mask over your mouth first and then the child's."

The last thing we are told is how many exits the plane is equipped with. Normally, there are four: one in front, two over the wings, and one in the rear of the plane. However, they always tell us to take note that the closest exit may be behind us. I don't know why, but, wow, that one really relaxes me. At that point, I settle into my seat, and from the moment the plane begins to taxi the runway I become drowsy. No matter how turbulent the flight, I can sleep from runway to runway.

The scientific term for this is "the white noise effect." Merriam-Webster's dictionary defines white noise as "a constant background noise; especially: one that drowns out other sounds or distractions."[1] However, white noise, also called white sound, is not a "noise." White noise is actually a sound frequency or a signal that we hear as a gentle hiss, similar to the sound of wind rustling through trees, a waterfall, radio static, or the ocean surf. It is constant and distinct.

In the pages of 1 Kings, there is a very familiar story about a prophet who had not yet learned to recognize God's frequency.

> *The LORD said, "Go out and stand on the mountain in the presence of the LORD, for the LORD is about to pass by." Then a great and powerful wind tore the mountains apart and shattered the rocks before the LORD, but the LORD was not in the wind. After the wind there was an earthquake, but the LORD was not in the earthquake. After the earthquake came a fire, but the LORD was not in the fire. And after the fire came a gentle whisper. When Elijah heard it, he pulled his cloak over his face and went out and stood at the mouth of the cave.*
>
> —1 KINGS 19:12-13 NIV

Elijah was a man of God, a powerful and respected prophet. His prayers had called down fire on Mount Carmel and shown all Israel that the Lord is God. Elijah had seen the power of God in ways that few human beings have ever seen. He was a man of prayer who walked with God and obeyed the Lord.

When God spoke to Elijah on Mount Horeb, He could have done so in the wind, earthquake, or fire. However, He did not. He spoke with a "still, small voice," as the King James Version puts it. God spoke to Elijah in a sound frequency that only he could recognized or discern. At that point in Elijah's life, he knew all about the big stuff, because God had used him to do mighty, spectacular things. Now God wanted him to understand that He could work in a different way. God wanted Elijah to learn to not just listen for the loud boom but to tune into the frequency of His quiet leading when the situation seemed hopeless. Quiet the noise.

> *God's voice is still and quiet and easily buried under an avalanche of clamor.*[2]
>
> —DR. CHARLES STANLEY

Just because there is no shout from heaven, that does not mean God is not speaking.

Finding God's frequency requires removing the noise and hindrances that keep us from hearing His voice. At the beginning of every year, in January, our church comes together for consecration. For the past few years our focus has been on the five senses (vision, hearing, smell, taste, and touch). When we got to the sense of hearing, our goal was to limit distractions, to quiet the noise, clutter, and busyness of our daily lives so that we could hear God more clearly.

How many times have we looked to God for answers in some loud and grand fireworks, not realizing that He speaks to us every single day as we allow His Word to permeate our hearts? God's Word is the primary vehicle He uses to transform minds, characters, and lives. The closer you get to Him, the easier it is for you to hear Him.

We must learn to hear above the noise to see that God speaks to us louder when we get quiet. We may not always hear God speak in an audible voice. Nevertheless, that does not mean God is not speaking to us. We must have our ears tuned to His frequency to catch the signal. Any impression we get, any voice we hear, any supposition or feeling we believe is the will of God must always be compared to what God has already said. For believers, the frequency He speaks at is His Word.

There are over seven billion people currently living in this world. Seven billion. And God chooses to speak, not just collectively to the whole of humanity, but to each of us individually. Expect to hear from God. Look for God. Be expectant, anticipating a word from Him at all times.

Chapter 4
Exhaust Him

Prayer can never be in excess.

-C.H. SPURGEON

It has been said that imitation is the sincerest form of flattery. To imitate means to copy or duplicate. It also means to mimic (impersonate), which is where we get our word *mime*.

Children learn through imitation. From language to social skills, most children in their first year learn by mimicking or imitating adults. They look and they listen. They will hear what you say, but they will mimic what you do. A mother smiles at her child, and the child smiles back. She squints up her nose and the child attempts to squint his nose. She sticks out her tongue and makes a sound; the child sticks out his tongue and blows bubbles trying to duplicate what he sees and hears. Young children process the information of a behavior and then practice it until it becomes second nature.

It is always inspiring to watch children imitate adults in worship. When they sing, they are so intense and their worship is so pure.

While sitting in the doctor's office once, I came across a small cartoon clip in a magazine. It showed a little girl standing next to her mom in church with her hands lifted in worship. The image in her mind of God was one of an old man sitting in a cloud with white hair and a white beard. The man also appears to be very tired. The cartoon caption read, "We Exhaust You, O Lord." Of course, if you are at all familiar with the song, you know the actual words are "We Exalt You, O Lord." This little girl presumed, based on what she heard and saw others do in worship, that our goal is to exhaust God with our constant singing and praising.

Imagine if it were true that we could exhaust God. What would that look like?

Webster's dictionary defines the word *exhaust* as "to drain, metaphorically; to use or expend wholly, or till the supply comes to an end; to deprive wholly of strength; to use up; to weary or tire out; to wear out; as, to exhaust one's strength, patience, or resources."[1] Just looking at the definition should tell us that it does not apply to our God. How do you deplete an infinite God of anything? This is just not possible.

In Isaiah 40, the prophet Isaiah records God's rhetorical question in response to Israel's obvious amnesia as to the kind of God they served.

> *Have you not known? Have you not heard? The everlasting God, the Lord, The Creator of the ends of the earth, neither faints nor is weary. His understanding is unsearchable. He gives power to the weak, and to those who have no might He increases strength.*
>
> —ISAIAH 40:28–29, NKJV

In *The Message* Bible, the passage reads: "Don't you know anything? Haven't you been listening? God doesn't come and go. God *lasts*. He's Creator of all you can see or imagine. He doesn't get tired out, doesn't pause to catch his breath. And he knows *everything*, inside and out. He energizes those who get tired, gives fresh strength to dropouts. For even young people tire and drop out, young folk in their prime stumble and fall. But those who wait upon GOD get fresh strength. They spread their wings and soar like eagles, they run and don't get tired, they walk and don't lag behind."

Everyone gets tired, young and old. We stumble and make mistakes. We tire from life, and each other when we have exceeded our capacity for emotional stress. We drop out, often ending relationships from mere emotional exhaustion. Many of us feel it, even when we are not aware that we have exhausted our emotional reserves.

The only cure for this type of exhaustion is to seek strength from an inexhaustible source.

Isaiah invites every believer to lean into what we already know about the Father. Our faith is strengthened not by something new but by coming back to what we have already heard and what we already know—that He is the giver and sustainer of life, and He will never tire of you.

What do you know about God? Has He made provisions for you? Has He been your protector? Your healer? Your strength? Everything He has been He will be again. God never gets tired of us needing Him. As Max Lucado wrote, no matter what our needs are, "we never exhaust God's supply."[2]

God never runs out of anything. Anything that is true about God is true without limits. He never runs out of resources, and He is not limited in any way. You may exhaust another individual's patience but God's is inexhaustible. The Lord does not tire. When God created all things in the space of six days, it did not tire Him and it was not a "rushed job." He rested only because He had finished His work. There is no situation that can ever come into your life that is too difficult or too complex for God to handle. God the Father is transcendent, and because of His vastness He is well capable of handling anything we can say or present to Him.

You can't exhaust His *strength*.

> *For it is [not your strength, but it is] God who is effectively at work in you, both to will and to work [that is, strengthening, energizing, and creating in you the longing and the ability to fulfill your purpose] for His good pleasure."*
>
> —PHILIPPIANS 2:13, AMP

You can't exhaust His *understanding*.

> *How great is God—beyond our understanding! The number of his years is past finding out.*
>
> —JOB 36:26, NRSV

You can't exhaust His *grace*.

> *But because of his great love for us, God, who is rich in mercy, made us alive with Christ even when we were dead in transgressions—it is by grace you have been saved.*
>
> —EPHESIANS 2:4–5, NIV

> *And God is able to make all grace abound to you, so that always having all sufficiency in everything, you may have an abundance for every good deed.*
>
> —2 CORINTHIANS 9:8, CEB

You can't exhaust *His love*.

> *Beloved, let us [unselfishly] love and seek the best for one another, for love is from God; and everyone who loves [others] is born of God and knows God [through personal experience]. The one who does not love has not become acquainted with God [does not and never did know Him], for God is love. [He is the originator of love, and it is an enduring attribute of His nature.]*
>
> —1 JOHN 4:7–8, AMP

> *But you, O Lord, are a God merciful and gracious, slow to anger and abounding in steadfast love and faithfulness.*
>
> —PSALM 86:15, NRSV

You can't exhaust *His provision*.

> *The LORD is my Shepherd [to feed, to guide and to shield me], I shall not want.*
>
> —PSALM 23:1, AMP

> *And my God will liberally supply (fill until full) your every need according to His riches in glory in Christ Jesus.*
>
> —PHILIPPIANS 4:19, AMP

We read in Psalm 121:4 that God never sleeps or slumbers. That means God is powerful and all-sufficient. He watches over His people, and He never sleeps. He doesn't close His eyes for a nap. He is watching always. A commentary I once read said God keeps a 24/7 watch over us and He doesn't need any coffee! We can never exhaust Him.

Chapter 5
Can Prayer Really Change This?

I don't pray to change God's mind, I pray to change my mind.

-C.S. LEWIS

There is a reason God refers to us as children in Scripture. Children, in all of their innocence, can also think they are the center of the universe. We can usually expect them to be selfish in their desires, concerned only with what their parents and others can do for them. You know that persistent whining, "Mommy, Mommy, Mommy, can I have this?" or "Daddy, can I have that?"

The truth is children whine because they feel helpless. Whining, they hope, will allow them to gain enough power to get their way. When self-centered people cannot get their way, whether child or adult, they will act out and whine. Whining has been classified as a personality disorder characterized by dramatic emotional behavior. As children mature into adolescence and adulthood, their way of thinking should be more giving and less self-centered. The whining should be almost nonexistent.

They should move from demanding to inquiring, "Mommy or Daddy, what can I do for you?"

While emotional maturity may be reflected in the quality of our relationships with people, spiritual maturity is reflected in the quality of our relationship with God. They go hand-in-hand.

Prayer is necessary to our spiritual growth and relationship with God. The problem is that most people measure the success and power of their prayers solely by what manifests physically. However, another true measure and testament to the power of prayer lies in our spiritual maturity—how we view our daily challenges, how well we navigate through life's difficulties, how we mediate conflicts, and how big we see our God in comparison to any obstacle.

On the flip side, a clear sign of immaturity is when what we want from God is more important than what we are willing to do for Him. It is when our prayers are about God doing our will and not about surrendering to His.

Early in my Christian walk, I was an extremely sensitive person. Even though I had the appearance of being strong, I was sensitive and easily wounded by the slightest hint of rejection. I constantly lamented to God about how people mistreated me—how they did not like me, how they continually talked about me. In all truth, I was a whiner. I would take my complaint to my pastor with confidence that he surely would call these agitators into his office and put an end to the whole mess. Not so!

My pastor was young but wise beyond his years. After listening to me attentively, he looked at me and said, "I want you to turn your plate down, and in your time of prayer and consecration, pray for these individuals." I thought to myself, "You have got to be kidding me! I just poured my heart out to you. You can see that I am hurting. Why in the world would you think the solution to my problem is for me to fast and pray for them?" Though outdone by his counsel, out of obedience, I did as he instructed.

For the first couple of days of my consecration, my prayers were short and insincere for the people I felt had wounded me and longer for myself. But as I continued to pray, something changed. By day three, instead of being self-centered, I found myself praying, "Father, please heal and bless my enemy. Show me their needs and concerns." Without realizing it, I was growing spiritually and could see that my whining was most definitely a sign of immaturity. My heart became tender, and my prayers moved from demanding my way to interceding for those individuals. Perhaps this is the reason Jesus told His disciples to "bless those who curse you, pray for those who mistreat you" (Luke 6:28, NIV). Was it really a lesson in the art of intercession?

Intercession is about more than just praying for ourselves or for someone else's needs. True intercession is praying with the real hope and real intent that God will step in and act in another person's favor. To intercede means to intervene on behalf of another. In other words, when you intercede for others, you are not just praying for them;

you are standing in the gap and praying for that person as if you were praying for yourself.

It's never about you.

The hardest thing to accept sometimes on this Christian journey is that it's really not about you. Yes, the way I was treated was unfair. Yes, it was an injustice. Yes, I believed there was an inequity. Nonetheless, we should never let our perception that an injustice has been done become an excuse to continue complaining.

Now, normally, we call people who we believe are attacking us *haters*. However, not everyone is your hater. Just as the enemy uses people to afflict you, sometimes God uses people to equip you. There is a vast difference between affliction and equipping. A prime example of this is found in the Book of Exodus.

In Exodus 9, God revealed to Pharaoh the true reason he had become such a prominent Egyptian ruler. He said, "But I have raised you up for this very purpose, that I might show you my power and that my name might be proclaimed in all the earth" (Exod. 9:16, NIV). The people of Israel may have felt they were being afflicted, but the entire time they were in Egypt, they were being equipped. Because of their experience, the world came to know the true and living God.

What if the attack you are experiencing is not there to destroy you but to motivate you to participate in the deliverance and healing of others? Perhaps God is giving you the credibility you need to minister with power and strength so that ultimately He will get the glory when people are set free.

Does our prayer change God's mind? No. God is unchangeable. He is not man. Dr. John R. W. Stott says this: "The purpose of prayer is emphatically not to bend God's will to ours, but rather to align our will to his".[1]

As we mature in our Christian walk, our hearts become enlarged and gain a greater capacity to understand who God is and a greater concern for what God requires. Most of us probably do not realize how much we get in the way of God's purpose for our lives. I thank God that my pastor saw in me what I could not see in myself.

There is no way you or I can have true horizontal relationships unless we have a true vertical relationship. When we have a good vertical relationship with our heavenly Father, it instills in us a desire to have good horizontal relationship with others that are not about meeting our own personal desires. Pastor Rick Warren once said, "God is far more interested in changing your mind than changing your circumstances."[2] Prayer may not change things, but it will certainly change you.

Whatever you are struggling with, confess it to a trusted spiritual friend and ask that person to pray for you. Write down a plan to revisit each issue after praying openly and honestly about it.

Is there something that is hindering your maturity? Let the Father deal with it. Give Him permission to speak into your life, and then act upon the word He gives you in obedience. It may be necessary to change your mind-set toward others and commit to praying for them. Praying for someone you may have difficulty with will expose any tendency to make everything about yourself.

We all have to grow up some time. Whatever it takes you to get there, do not be afraid to submit to His will. Stop whining and celebrate maturity! God wants to work the challenges you're facing together for your good!

Chapter 6
Don't Play With Your Weakness

With a leap he stood upright and began to walk; and he entered the temple with them, walking and leaping and praising God.

—ACTS 3:8, NASB

Do you remember what it was like when you were a child and you wanted to get something down from high up but you couldn't quite reach it? You'd start by lifting yourself up on your tippy toes. When that failed, you would jump and jump, stretching your arms up as high as possible hoping to grasp the item with your fingers. When that didn't work, you would start to think to yourself, "If only I had someone to give me a boost, then maybe I could reach it." So you would ask a sibling, a friend, or an adult to help. For the boost, they would lift you up or let you climb on their shoulders while giving you a good push up. This gave you just the extra edge needed to get what you were reaching for.

However, even though the boost gave you an edge, it solved your problem only for the moment. The next time you needed to reach something up high, you would have to ask someone for the same assistance.

In high school, I was part of the girls' basketball team. Despite being only 5 feet tall, I had strong arms and legs. I was quick, which made me good at stealing the ball. The element of surprise was that I could shoot the ball at half court and make it! Of course, that was in the girls' high school gymnasium. I credit much of my ability to a great high school gym teacher and coach, Ms. Jean Owens, who was relentless.

The girls on most of the teams we played were bigger and stronger than we were. We could not take them one-on-one. It was a challenge even to get a shot off because they would block them every time. Our coach's strategy was to teach us how to play to our strengths while challenging our weak areas.

What we needed was that extra boost to help us make the basket from farther out. But our coach could not pick us up by the knees and lift us up to reach the basket. Coach laid out an exercise program that involved strengthening techniques (squats, layups, running laps, pushups, etc.). This was an attempt to improve our "vertical reach" or "vertical jump."

We learned what every good player knows. Our vertical reach had nothing to do with how tall we were; we just had to be able to lift our bodies high enough for the activity.

The quickest way to jump higher is to focus your vertical jump training on your areas of weakness. In practically every sport, the vertical leap is frequently used as a tool to measure a player's power and strength, and how well that player could use his or her strength. Coaches can look at a player's vertical jump and immediately know how explosive of an athlete they have on their hands.

In the kingdom, prayer is a measuring tool to assess our ability to operate effectively and to display the explosive power and strength of the Holy Spirit in our lives. In Acts 3:1–26, as Peter and John journeyed to the temple to pray, they meet a lame man.

> *One day Peter and John were going up to the temple at the time of prayer—at three in the afternoon. Now a man who was lame from birth was being carried to the temple gate called Beautiful, where he was put every day to beg from those going into the temple courts. When he saw Peter and John about to enter, he asked them for money. Peter looked straight at him, as did John. Then Peter said, "Look at us!" So the man gave them his attention, expecting to get something from them. Then Peter said, "Silver or gold I do not have, but what I do have I give you. In the name of Jesus Christ of Nazareth, walk." Taking him by the right hand, he helped him up, and instantly the man's feet and ankles became strong. He jumped to his feet and began to walk. Then he went with them into the temple courts, walking and jumping, and praising God.*
>
> —Acts 3:1-9

For over forty years this man suffered from an ailment which made him lame. The writer tells us he was born that way. A possibly birth defect. He had never known the freedom of going anywhere without getting others to carry him there. This man had been a beggar for many, if not most, of those forty-plus years. We know he was carried daily to his station at the gate of the temple. A gate identified as the "Beautiful" gate. As Peter and John were heading toward or into the temple, the lame man was being carried to his normal post, at the gate. The man was not sitting or lying down at the gate but on his way. As he is approaching his station, he observes Peter and John nearby about to go into the temple. However, it was not the beggar who fixed his eyes on Peter and John, but they who first fixed their eyes on him. Looking at the man, Peter says, "Look at us!". The man looked reluctantly not sure what to expect, if anything, from them. But it was evident that they fully intended to do something for him.

They did not have money to give him, but they had something better. They gave what they had, and it turned out to be explosive. As Peter reached to help him up, he uses the authority of the name of Jesus. Then Peter and John watch as the power of healing transfers from Peter's hands, straight through the man's body, to the man's feet and ankles. It gave him the strength to stand. Then to leap. Then to praise the Lord.

The man went from a horizontal position and relying on the kindness of strangers to a vertical position of pulling on the strength of God. The man no longer used his weakness as a means of making a living. He was so excited to be able to use his legs that he ran, leaping and dancing throughout the city so that everyone could see his transformation.

In Christendom, we are often told not to concentrate on our weakness but to operate from our strengths. However, we have to acknowledge our weak areas and keep them before God. Otherwise, we will default to our weakness every time we face an obstacle. He makes us strong where we are weak. God makes up for our deficits. That's why the Lord told Paul "...My grace is sufficient for thee: for my strength is made perfect in weakness. Most gladly therefore will I rather glory in my infirmities, that the power of Christ may rest upon me" (2 Cor. 12:9, KJV).

God wants to use you despite your weaknesses, imperfections, limitations, and insecurities. We must strengthen our weak areas by building our vertical reach to God. There is an explosive power at work in you for all to see. As you go to God in prayer, expect Him to hear you and to answer according to His will.

Chapter 7
24/7

For through him we both have access to the Father by one Spirit.

-EPHESIANS 2:18, NIV

It is exciting when you have friends in high places, especially when those friends are in the music or television industry. Whenever you are their guest at a special event, you receive special access backstage because you have badges with the words VIP or "All Access" written on them. This pass gives you unrestricted admittance to all the activities of the event.

In everyday life, there are places where access is denied. Some private properties have NO TRESPASSING signs. Certain doors in airports, hospitals, and government buildings have signs with big bold letters that say AUTHORIZED PERSONNEL ONLY, indicating general access is prohibited. Therefore, if you work or live in any of these places, your access to certain areas may be limited. To those who are authorized to enter those restricted areas, there is nothing secretive about what is happening behind those doors. But the public is left to wonder.

The agency I work for shares a building with other companies, so my employer requires that we carry identification badges at all times. Those badges give us access to all areas of our agency and keep us secure during and after business hours. One evening I was working late on a project and when I finished up, I stopped in the ladies' room before heading out to meet my husband for dinner. The restrooms are located in the lobby area on the opposite end of the building, which means we need our badges in order to gain access to our office area when we return.

As always, I grabbed my badge and headed down the long hall, through the doors, into the lobby, and to the restrooms. When I returned to enter the doors of our offices, I placed my ID card at the security pad and pulled the knob. The pad beeped, but I was not able to open the door. Thinking nothing more than that I must not have had my badge positioned at the pad correctly, I turned it around and again placed it at the security pad and pulled the doorknob. Once again nothing opened.

Suddenly a light went on in my head, and I thought to myself, "What time is it?" It was 7 p.m., but I knew I had twenty-four-hour access.

I had a problem. I was in a common area but could not exit the building to seek help or get to my car. My purse, car keys, and cell phone were all locked in my office, which was in an area I could not access. How was I going to get out?

After a brief conversation with myself, I heard the cleaning crew moving around on the next level. I went to locate them and asked them to let me into my office area so I could get my things. Then I thought, "Isn't this ironic? I am an employee and I can't gain access to my office after a certain hour, but the cleaning crew, who doesn't work for the agency, has access to my area twenty-four hours a day."

I had not realized that I did not have twenty-four-hour access, because I had never needed to use it until then.

Noncompliance will forfeit your access.

The next day, I contacted our IT department to find out why my badge would not work after a certain time. I was informed that my badge should have given me twenty-four-hour access, but I had not responded to a recent memorandum to have it upgraded. Access was made available to me, but I missed it because I ignored the invitation.

How many times have you missed an important notice, a free opportunity, or a check in the mail because it did not look important enough to open? We take for granted the access we have to the Father because of and through Christ. When we pray to the Father, because of Christ we can ask anything of Him and be assured that He will grant our petition.

Author and preacher E.M. Bounds once wrote, "None but the earnest man gets access to the ear of God."[1] To have access to something means you have a right of entry or use in a spiritual or natural sense. It means to have "free admission."

As followers of Christ, there are things we have access to, things that are readily made available to us. One of these things is that we have free admission, or "all access," to God's presence. This means we have no restraints, no restrictions, and no required reservations. It does not cost us a thing to come into God's presence and we do not need an escort.

Paul writes to the Ephesians about this access. He says:

> *This in accordance with [the terms of] the eternal purpose which He carried out in Christ Jesus our Lord, in whom we have boldness and confident access through faith in Him [that is, our faith gives us sufficient courage to freely and openly approach God through Christ].*
>
> –EPHESIANS 3:11–12, AMP

Sometimes we forget the things God has given us access to. When we think we need authority, all we really need is access, because God has given us the freedom to choose to access His power. Our spiritual power source comes from listening and communicating with God. Faith in Jesus should give us boldness, confidence, and access. It is our faith that allows us to access whatever we need for our lives.

If we are in Christ and we exercise our faith by believing God and His Word, we can get access to what we need. You may not have it right now, but by knowing God and His Word, you can find out how to get there. When you know how to get there, you can walk in "God confidence," knowing that even if you don't have the full manifestation of what you need, it will come.

Prayer is a doorway into the presence of God. It is an access point. Through faith and the power of prayer, we have access to the power to change things, hearts, and systems, and affect spiritual atmospheres. We have unlimited access to the throne of God, where we can get to know what God is speaking and doing. Everything you need is within your reach.

Chapter 8
What Could Be Better?

"Martha, Martha," the Lord answered, "you are worried and upset about many things, but few things are needed—or indeed only one. Mary has chosen what is better, and it will not be taken away from her."

—LUKE 10:41–42, NIV

There is a running joke in my family about my youngest sibling and me. It is said, for good reason, that she is Martha and I am Mary. Whenever we have a family gathering, she is always stressed and concerned with what other people are going to contribute to the meal. Frankly, I tend to stay out of the kitchen, because they think I am not capable of preparing a dish to their liking. I am not offended, though. The less I boast about being able to do, the less I have to do.

A family event should always be enjoyable to everybody who attends. However, when we are caught up in the event, losing sight of its intended purpose, it can become most frustrating. My family's dynamics are much like many other families'. We all have hectic lives doing this and that in our personal, church, and professional sphere. So it is a rare treasure when the entire family has the opportunity to sit down, catch up, and share a meal. For me, these times are all about spending time with my family. For my sister, much like Martha, they are all about the meal—which everyone appreciates!

In Luke 10, we find that Martha is the epitome of hospitality. Probably nervous with excitement over the opportunity to host Jesus, Martha wanted everything to be just right. Can you imagine a greater privilege than being able to serve a meal to Jesus and His disciples? Martha needed some help, and her sister Mary was nowhere to be found. Finally she finds her sitting at the feet of Jesus, listening to Him teach.

If Mary and Martha's family was anything like mine, there was probably plenty of melodrama when Martha found her sister. I can imagine Martha standing in the corner of the room calling Mary in a nice-nasty way, demanding that she come and assist her in preparing and cleaning up the meal. I can see Mary purposely ignoring her, causing Martha to address Jesus.

Martha's complaint to Jesus over her sister's lack of help prompted one of the most radical statements Jesus ever spoke. If we allow His words to sink into our lives, we will be forever changed. "Martha, Martha," He said, "you are worried and upset about many things, but only one thing is needed." Then He pointed to what Mary was doing as the one thing.

I cannot imagine how that may have made Martha feel, but I am sure Mary felt relieved. We know that Jesus was not discounting Martha's service. Thank God, my sister loves to cook, because if the food were left up to me we would probably have nothing but chips and dip at our family gatherings. But Jesus did not want Martha to lose sight of the purpose of His presence. It is almost like He was saying, "Martha, this is a rare moment for you to be this close and this intimate with Me. You should treasure this time with Me, not spend it in the kitchen."

Most of us are extremely busy with many activities that seem necessary. Our calendars are full of things that we think are important and should be done. However, in the midst of our horizontal activity, only one thing is truly essential. How do we become so busy with life that we forget to spend time with the One who gives life?

Amazingly, the "one thing" Mary was engaged in did not require her to really do anything! She was simply being with Jesus and preferring this to everything else she could have been occupied with on that particular day. In Luke 10, Jesus is gently telling us that being with Him is the one thing we should commit ourselves to—above everything else.

What is your priority? Listen to the vertical compass of your heart. Embrace what is needed. Look to Jesus. Be determined to have not just an experience with Him, but an encounter. As I heard evangelist Robert Madu say once, "When Jesus is not intimately known, He cannot be accurately shown."

Jesus redirects us from a horizontal lifestyle that focuses on our personal needs; our personal circle of friends and family; our agendas, budgets, and seemingly endless list of "important" activities toward a vertical posture that fixes our eyes on His love, His purpose, and His presence, just as it was with Mary.

Part II
Vertical Focus

Worship will get you through the roughest times in your life, because it shifts your focus from the problem to the problem solver!

-Author Unknown

Chapter 9
Vertical Focus

Set your minds on things that are above, not on things are on earth.

-COLOSSIANS 3:2, ESV

Setting our minds on things above is what I call having a vertical focus. It means we cultivate a pattern of looking to God each day to learn His agenda for our lives.

Whether we realize it or not, we often are more focused on the horizontal things around us than on looking to the Father. We may want to live a vertical life, with our minds and hearts focused on things above, but we easily tilt to the horizontal, allowing ungodly spiritual forces to capture our thoughts, actions, and focus.

We do our best to center our attention on Christ, but the truth of the matter is earthly things distract us. They are shiny and tempting. They cause us to take wrong exits and stay too long at rest stops. If we are to be certain we are in line with Colossians 3:2, we must regularly step back and take inventory of our spiritual walk and our prayer lives.

Oftentimes, it is not the big things but the small things that tilt our focus away from God. Song of Solomon 2:15 speaks of the little foxes that eat at the vine and destroy the grapes while they are tender. *Whatever you allow to keep your attention you allow to keep you.*

When I look back at the times I lost focus in my prayer life, I realize that it happened a little at a time. Whether it was concentrating on a relationship, a job, or finances, the more engulfed I became in my venture, the less time I seemed to commit to prayer.

I can remember becoming so consumed with an individual at one time in my life that every conversation, good or bad, became about that person. Out of concern for me, a friend tenderly said, "Deb, you've lost your focus." She was right. Something that could have been a blessing in my life suddenly became the one thing that was cursing my relationship with the Father.

The one thing that has your attention could be keeping you from fulfilling God's predetermined plan for your life. You may not even notice how far you have gone, but God will give you warning signs. Never ignore them or the voice of reason.

Chapter 10
Distractions

> *Whatever excites the curiosity scatters the thoughts, disquiets the heart, absorbs the interests or shifts our life focus from the kingdom of God within us to the world around us—that is a distraction; and the world is full of them.*
>
> —A.W. TOZER

Siegfried Fischbacher and Roy Horn, better known as Siegfried & Roy, are most famous for their Las Vegas performances with white lions and white tigers. However, decades ago there was another famous lion tamer named Clyde Beatty.

Clyde Beatty was born in Bainbridge, Ohio, in 1903. When he was a teenager, he left home to join the circus and landed a job as a cage cleaner. In the years that followed, Beatty quickly progressed from a lowly cage boy to a popular entertainer.[1]

Beatty became famous for his "fighting act," in which he would tame fierce wild animals. On one occasion,

Beatty's act included a segment where he brought lions, tigers, cougars, and hyenas into the circus ring all at once and tamed the entire group.[2] He was also one of the first lion tamers to bring a chair into the circus ring.

The classic image of a lion tamer is one of the entertainer holding a gun, a whip, and a chair. They have a gun in case the lion is out of control. They would shoot in the air (gun was filled with blanks) to regain control. They had a whip supposedly to call the attention of the lion. The whip gets all of the attention, but it's mostly for show. In reality, it's the chair that does the important work.[3]

As author James Clear wrote, "When a lion tamer holds a chair in front of the lion's face, the lion tries to focus on all four legs of the chair at the same time. With its focus divided, the lion becomes confused and is unsure about what to do next. When faced with so many options, the lion gets distracted and chooses to freeze and wait instead of attacking the man holding the chair."[4]

At a time when the majority of lion tamers died in the ring, Beatty lived into his sixties. In the end, it was cancer that took his life, not a lion.[5]

The application here is that distractions will paralyze you.

There is certainly no shortage of distractions in life. They are a universal obstacle. Watching television and surfing the Internet can keep people entertained and distracted for hours at a time. Then there are games and gadgets, work and cell phones. It's a wonder we ever get anything done.

To be distracted is to have our attention diverted. To divert means "to turn from one course or use to another."[6] Distractions cause delays because they get you off the desired course or direction. This makes them detrimental to your destiny.

Sometimes we put ourselves in situations where we will be distracted. We kneel to pray and our cell phones are on. Our laptops or iPad are nearby. This would make it difficult for anyone to concentrate. So how do we overcome distractions that seek to divert our attention from prayer? How do we keep the pressures of life from diverting our attention during the difficult times? What do we do when we need help and God does not seem to be answering our prayers?

The first step in overcoming is to acknowledge that distractions will surface during our prayer times and vie for our attention. When we come into prayer, there will be times in all of our lives when we will have to wage spiritual war just so we can concentrate fully on the Father.

There are generally two types of distractions that you will war against in prayer. The first is *voluntary* distractions. A voluntary distraction occurs when a thought comes to mind and you began to dwell on it. Say for instance that you are going to buy a new car. You try to pray, but you turn your attention away from God, thinking about that shiny new car. You choose to think about that car instead of spending time in prayer. That distraction is voluntary.

Voluntary distractions can do a lot of damage to your prayer life. In essence, you are saying, "God, You are not as important to me right now as this car I'm planning to buy." Distractions reveal to us what we are attached to. In other words, you are distracted in prayer because your heart is divided.

God will not compete with that, and He will not take away your voluntary distraction. That, my friend, is on you! He wants us to choose Him over the other things vying for our affection, and that is no easy task. Getting past voluntary distractions takes discipline, willpower, focus, and faith. In order to avoid these voluntary distractions, you must surrender your whole heart to the Father.

The second type of distraction is *involuntary*. These are things you did not invite, things you don't necessarily want to think about—work or family obligations, or projects in which you may be involved. These distractions just come at you, which is why you must take on the mind of a warrior. Turn your attention back to God by concentrating solely on the task at hand—prayer. You have the ability to control your own attention.

When in prayer, learn to remove and refuse. Remove your attention from everything except God, and keep it there by refusing to allow any thoughts entrance into your mind except thoughts about the Father. Spending time in worship helps with this. Worship puts our focus on the Father, and He becomes so captivating that distractions cannot enter.

Chapter 11
Waterfalls

Deep calls to deep in the roar of your waterfalls.

—PSALM 42:7, NIV

Most mornings when I awake, there is a song on my heart. At times, it is a melody to encourage me throughout my day; at other times, it is a song developing into notes of inspiration for others. On one particular morning I woke up with a secular song in my head. The song was "Waterfalls" by the female R&B group TLC. I know. It was not "Jesus Be a Fence," but before you judge, hear me out.

It has been my experience, having great compassion and a strong desire to see people set free, that certain experiences will move you to reflect on things you have seen or heard. You may read a particular quote or hear a certain song, and it will remind you of people and pleasures you should have been delivered from long ago.

A waterfall is a flow of water over the edge of a cliff. Waterfalls are awe-inspiring as you watch the water cascade down the side of a mountain and flow into a bubbling stream. They are easy to visualize even if you have never seen one. I love the serenity of waterfalls. They stimulate my spiritual senses and ignite my creativity. They have the ability to draw me closer to the God of all creation.

Waterfalls can be so captivating, I forget all about the cares of the outside world when I'm watching one. And the longer I watch, the more captivating it becomes. Then I start to wonder, "How does it do that? Where does it start? Where does it go? Is there an end?" Waterfalls move me from inspiration to deliberation in seconds and cause me to long for more understanding.

The song "Waterfalls" reflected socially conscious lyrics. It was TLC's way of expressing how people chase intangible dreams with no thought of the consequences. The first verse is talking about the relationship between an inner-city mother and her son. He is chasing *waterfalls* (money and respect by dealing drugs), but his mother knows this cannot end well. The second verse deals with a man's relationship with a woman. His *waterfall* is casual sex—he has a "natural obsession for temptation." He contracts HIV and dies ("three letters took him to his final resting place").

Though the song was dead-on, we have no real evidence that it was able to make a significant impact on its culture. What we do know is the Bible has consistently spoken to us about being responsible, not by using condoms but by resisting the temptation to engage in high-risk activity because it will bring deadly consequences, spiritually, physically, or both.

> *But each one is tempted when he is dragged away, enticed and baited [to commit sin] by his own [worldly] desire (lust, passion). Then when the illicit desire has conceived, it gives birth to sin; and when sin has run its course, it gives birth to death.*
>
> —JAMES 1:14–15, AMP

My brother was only twenty-six years old when he was murdered. His *waterfall* was money. He had been a midlevel distributor of illegal pharmaceutical goods (a drug dealer). Six months before he died, he gave his life to the Lord and became a member of the church my sister and I attended. He had done a complete one-eighty in his life—giving up the quick money, the women, and the drugs. He ate the Word and cultivated a life of prayer and fasting. We were so proud of what God was doing through him.

But after a while, he began to miss the money. It was difficult for him to work for $4.50 an hour when he was used to having thousands of dollars in his pocket. He began to struggle within. When he wanted to do what was good, evil showed up and made demands on him. (See Romans 7:21–25, AMP.) His thought pattern was that if only he could make one more score, he would be set and not have to worry about money for a while. And that thinking led to his demise.

The pressures of *if only* can weary the mightiest individual. My brother wanted more. He knew there was more to have. But he did not know how to obtain it.

Bible teacher Watchman Nee once wrote, "Only a call from the depths can provoke a response from the depths."[1] The theologians Blaise Pascal and St. Augustine have both been credited with saying there is a God-shaped vacuum in our hearts—a hole that only God can fill. If we try to put anything else in there, it will not fit, meaning it will not fill the need we have inside our heart and soul. In Psalm 42:7, the psalmist describes this feeling as simply overwhelming: "Deep calls to deep at the sound of Your waterfalls" (NASB).

When we come into God's presence in prayer, there is a depth in God that we are trying to commune with. However, in order to get where He is from where we are, we must call to God from the depth of our souls. We cannot be superficial in our prayer life and become disappointed when things do not turn out as we had hoped.

I was despondent for some years after losing my brother. I often wondered if I had done all I could to encourage him to stay the course. Did I love him enough? Did I pray for him hard enough? To comfort me, the Lord took me in a vision and allowed me to walk into what appeared to be the very room where my brother had been murdered. I could see him tied up in a chair while they beat and taunted him. I heard him plead for his life, saying, "Please, I have a little girl".

As I stood watching and crying in the vision, I could hear the voice of the Lord say to me, "I am a just God." He said nothing more. From that day forward, I would be comforted by the words of 2 Thessalonians 1:6: "God is just: He will pay back trouble to those who trouble you" (NIV). I knew that no matter how many "if onlys" I could think of, none of them would ever compare to the comfort of knowing how much the Father loved my brother.

The enemy wants us to believe that "if only" we had these *things*, then our lives would be complete. He shows us the upside in big bold letters, but the consequences are in the tiny print at the bottom of the page. The bottom line is that every created thing will ultimately fail. Whether it is a person, position, possession, or property, they all have the potential to fail you. "The grass dries up, the flowers wither, but the decree of our God is forever reliable" (Is. 40:8, NET BIBLE). The only true failure is a failure to trust God.

It is extremely difficult to plan your life according to the world's system and ideal of success. No matter what you do, no matter where you go, you will probably never have enough of that *one thing* you so desire outside of the Father. Many times what we want is not a bad thing, but the desire to have it can consume us. Check yourself. Is what you're seeking what God wants for your life? Put your trust in its rightful place. Seek His face and not His hand. Wait for God. It is His delight to give you good gifts, as His Word says, "And my God will liberally supply (fill until full) your every need according to His riches in glory in Christ Jesus" (Phil. 4:19, AMP).

Chapter 12
Hitting the Wall!

Keep your eyes straight ahead; ignore all sideshow distractions.

—PROVERBS 4:25–27, THE MESSAGE

When my siblings and I were young, my family loved to go to the funny car and stock car races. We would watch from the stands for hours as the cars circled the track. In some race classes, the participants were not professional drivers. Therefore, every driver received instruction before going out onto the track.

One of the first things they would tell them was not what to do, but rather what to focus on should they go into a tailspin. They would tell them that if they tried to avoid hitting the wall, they would usually wind up hitting it, because avoiding the wall meant the driver would have to focus on it. Instead, they were instructed to focus on where they wanted to go. By doing that, they would stand a better chance of avoiding the wall and successfully getting out of the spin.

Avoiding the wall can mean the difference between life and death. Amanda Gambacorto was a twenty-one-year-old marketing intern from Middletown, N.J., who was double-majoring in environmental humanities and philosophy at Stony Brook University. Described as bubbly and friendly, she was good, hard-working, and smart. She had a lot of friends and big plans for her life.

One Saturday, she decided to participate in a racing clinic called the Green Flag Driving Experience. The clinic attracted people who wanted to know what it was like to get behind the wheel of a racecar. With her hands firmly grasping the steering wheel, Amanda followed another vehicle around the track, but as they approached the "notorious" second turn at the stadium, Amanda began to lose control of her vehicle. Considered "inexperienced," she spun out of control and struck a wall. Sadly, Amanda's life plans would not be realized. She was pronounced dead from massive head trauma at the hospital less than an hour after the crash.[1]

I cannot begin to imagine what may have gone through Amanda's mind as she spun out of control on that dreadful day. Every time drivers race the potential exists for as many cars to crash as cross the finish line. The only difference between those who crash and those who finish intact is their focus. *Where your focus goes, your life will follow.*

Bishop Dale C. Bronner, an Atlanta-area pastor, once said, "Distraction is the destruction of your dream in slow motion."[2] Just as it is on the racetrack, our lives can spin out of control when we lack focus. Our lives have a tendency to move in the direction of our focus. And the same is true of our prayer lives.

What's distracting you? Once you identify it, be determined to remove and refuse every type of distraction. Focus and refocus, and you will not have to worry about hitting the wall. Whatever you focus on today in prayer, you give that thing permission to exist tomorrow.

That means it may be time to refocus. Even after we reorder our life to become vertically focused on God, we can expect to have the same life problems everyone else encounters. However, our experiences should differ from a person with only a horizontal focus. Be careful not to allow ungodly advice from peers, coworkers, or family members to influence your decision-making.

To refocus, you may have to isolate yourself for a while. Plan some time in solitude with limited distractions. You will find that when you tap into the God-given desires of your heart, you will experience change. Your time will be focused. Your energy will be focused. Your spiritual activity will be focused, and you will become a much more productive person.

It's a good practice to ask God for a fresh revelation and understanding of who He is and what He wants you to do. If you focus on God's dreams, goals, and vision for your life, and on where you want to be, not where you came from or the barriers ahead, then you will find yourself right on course. Set your eyes straight ahead on Jesus, the pioneer and perfecter of our faith, and FOCUS: Follow One Course Until Successful!

Part III
Vertical View in Distress, Grief, and Loss

He never said; you will not be troubled—you will not be tempted—you will not be distressed. But He said: you will not be overcome. (ISAIAH 43:2)

—Juliana of Norwich

Chapter 13
Life Hurts

Then call on me when you are in trouble, and I will rescue you.

—PSALM 50:15, NLT

Remember when you were a kid and you skinned your knee and asked your mother to kiss it and make it well? Wouldn't it be great if all the hurts of life could be healed with a mother's kiss? Let's face it, life hurts. Many people think they are unique when they are experiencing severe personal pain. They think their distress is unique, that their grief is one-of-a-kind, that no one could understand their loss on any level.

There is a saying, "When a person loses hope, they begin to hope for death." If you ever felt like just giving up, you are not alone. David once penned these words in a time of despair:

> *Oh, that I had wings like a dove! I would fly away and be at rest. I would wander far away, I would lodge in the [peace of the] wilderness. Selah. I would hurry to my refuge [my tranquil*

> *shelter far away] from the stormy wind and from the tempest.*
>
> —PSALM 55:6–8, AMP

That really tells a story of taking the easy way out. Who hasn't looked for one? It's been almost thirty years since I met with my pastor about the calling I felt upon my life. I can remember how elated he was to impart his wisdom and counsel to me. He spoke over me with prophetic insight. His words were, "You will stand to speak, and the words from your mouth will touch lives as though you are seeing directly into their hearts. Your message will be a message that relates, bringing healing and deliverance. When you share your story and experiences, people will come to you and tell you that you were speaking directly to their present circumstance." Those prophetic words have remained true to this day. When I first stood to open my mouth, no one but the Father knew my pain. But He has used my pain to minister healing others.

So many people throw their hands up in despair when their problems seem beyond their control. Perhaps you are going through something in your life that has you literally squeezed between two things. You might be dealing with a situation where it seems you'll make the wrong decision no matter how you choose to respond. Maybe you are just about to call it quits because it seems the more you pray, the worse things become. The enemy tells you that you are defeated and that you have no real purpose, and he is flooding your mind with thoughts of hopelessness and suicide.

Perhaps you have been facing such a lengthy trial that you do not believe you can endure much longer. You are tempted to lose heart because you just cannot see through the fog of your difficulty. Even though you may feel as if you are experiencing problem after problem or tragedy after tragedy, trust that they are not intended to kill you but will bring good in your life and be used to shift you into your purpose and destiny.

The truth is, we live in a broken world. So it stands to reason that at some point in our lives, whether it's through rejection, betrayal, or shame, we will experience pain and brokenness. But I'm a firm believer that God can't work through us what He has not already worked in us.

If God established a plan for your life before the challenges came into play, then He has already made provision to help you endure. He knows the anger and pain you feel, the times when you considered giving up, and even the times when you did! In order to reach your God-ordained, predetermined destiny, it is imperative that you learn to believe that God is in control.

When you feel like giving up, remember why you held on for so long in the first place.

Chapter 14
Lord, Keep My Mind!

You will keep in perfect peace those whose minds are steadfast, because they trust in you.

—ISAIAH 26:3, NIV

Life is full of assaults on our mind. Perhaps you have heard the saying, "If it's not one thing, it's another or the same thing." This is why it is imperative that we are always in a posture of prayer. I don't mean that we must literally lay out all day in prayer, but we must have our hearts and minds open to pray about everything in every situation at all times.

My life would be consumed by a series of events resulting in loss. It is what I term "my trilogy of tragedy." In one year I lost a child, my brother was brutally murdered, and my marriage fell apart. In a very dark hour, the spirit of grief took over my heart. One particular day while I was travelling on the interstate, I was crying so profusely the road in front of me became barely visible.

Although I was moving at top speed, I never felt like I was losing control of my vehicle. But I could hear the enemy try to seize the opportunity. He said, "Go ahead.

Let the wheel go. No one will know. They will believe it was an accident." For one split second, his words made sense to me. Suddenly becoming aware that I was about to lose control of my vehicle, I did the one thing we have been taught to do when in trouble, I called on the name of Jesus. At that moment, my car slowed down. It was as if someone steered it from behind and guided it to the side of the road.

I am living proof that there is power in the name of Jesus. Not only was my life spared, but the assault on my mind was instantly broken.

God's promise in the chaos is that *He will keep your mind* and your peace will be perfect. The Hebrew word for both perfect and peace is shalom, which figuratively means well, happy, and friendly and abstractly means welfare, as in one's health, prosperity, and peace.[1] So the text is saying, "I will keep him in peace, peace who minds is fixed." It's like saying you will have a double portion of peace. However, you have to choose it.

First, you have to trust in Him. "Trust in the Lord with all your heart..." Proverbs 3:5

Trusting God is simply believing that He loves you, He's good, He has the power to help you, He wants to help you, and He will help you. Instead of relying on our own knowledge, perception, or reasoning, we should put our total trust in the Lord. This requires more than just agreeing with Him. Agreement means we believe something is right. We can actually agree with God's word without actually trusting Him. When we truly trust God it means we don't get to pick and choose areas we entrust to Him while trying to keep other parts of our lives under our control. Even when we don't understand or like what's happening in our lives, our part is to respond in trust.

Corrie ten Boom and her sister Betsy were sent to a Nazi concentration camp because her family hid Jews during World War II. Betsy died in that camp, but Corrie was released.[2] After the war, she traveled the world, telling people about God's love. Corrie knew first-hand how difficult life can be. But she said, "Never be afraid to trust an unknown future to a known God."[3]

Second, you have to keep your mind fixed on Him, without doubting and without wavering.

Your mind is the greatest gift God has given you and it ought to be devoted entirely to Him. If we allow it to, our mind can and will, work against us. You should seek to be "bringing every thought into captivity to the obedience of Christ…" (2 Corinthians 10:5). This will be one of the greatest assets of your faith when a time of trial comes, because then your faith and the Spirit of God will work together.

> *"Brothers and sisters, continue to think about what is good and worthy of praise. Think about what is true and honorable and right and pure and beautiful and respected.*
>
> —Philippians 4:8 ERV

I wish I could say that was the end of the attacks. It was not! The difference between my reaction before my deliverance and afterward was that the enemy no longer had control of my mind. I knew the authority I possessed and that I had the power to speak to my thoughts and bring them under subjection to God.

The Bible says, "For the weapons of our warfare are not carnal but mighty in God for pulling down strongholds, casting down arguments and every high thing that exalts itself against the knowledge of God, bringing every thought into captivity to the obedience of Christ" (2 Cor. 10:4–5, NKJV). I challenge you to speak life to yourself and to those you feel are about to call it quits. *Rest if you must, but don't quit!*

Chapter 15
A Message for Your Womb

Shall I bring to the point of birth and not cause to bring forth?" says the Lord; "shall I, who cause to bring forth, shut the womb?" says your God.

—ISAIAH 66:9, ESV

It happens through children, coworkers, neighbors, friends, random passers-by, or even billboards. I am inspired and encouraged in many ways throughout the day. On one particular day, I was deeply moved while listening to an inspirational radio station.

A young woman was sharing her testimony of how God brought her through a recent miscarriage. As she shared the account of what was to be a routine prenatal visit, I held my breath as I anticipated her next words. When the doctor performed the sonogram, she anxiously looked over at the instruments and the sonogram screen. This was supposed to be an exciting day, but nothing could have prepared her for what would happen next.

Her doctor stopped in the middle of the test and said, "Just know that if there is something wrong, it's not your fault." She suddenly realized there was no heartbeat. What she saw on the screen was not the picture of a healthy, growing baby, but of a lifeless child. Even with the physician's words of reassurance, she still questioned what had she done to cause this.

Her story triggered memories of the many losses I had experienced in my life, and I began to feel a familiar pain in my chest. As the woman continued, all I could do was think to myself, "Yes, I know." I remembered often feeling that I had miscarried because I had done something wrong, and I searched and searched for a rhyme or reason for my loss.

When women find themselves experiencing a miscarriage, they will question everything they know to be true. They will think, "Perhaps it was something I did in my past that caused this to happen. Maybe God is punishing me. Maybe something is wrong with me. Why can't my body carry a child?" It's hard enough when you begin to question your ability to reproduce, but it's even more painful when you have to repeat your loss to others.

Yet we have to face our pain, even when it's invisible. The Bible says:

> *In the same way I will not cause pain without allowing something new to be born," says the LORD. "If I cause you the pain, I will not stop you from giving birth to your new nation," says your God.*
>
> —ISAIAH 66:9, NCV

The truth of the matter is that many things happen in life that are not our fault. Our lives are full of challenges that have nothing to do with anything we have done. Neither this young woman nor I had done anything wrong. Miscarriages happen more often than we think. Statistically speaking, 10 to 15 percent of pregnancies end in miscarriage, and each year roughly 1 percent of babies are stillborn.[1]

Many women experience the loss of a child or suffer a miscarriage, and the pain it renders is almost indescribable. It truly leaves you inconsolable, and it can be hard to understand because there is no physical injury you can use to measure the pain. When someone breaks a leg, suffers a severe burn, or is covered with cuts and bruises, it is easy for people to see what is wrong and to sympathize. However, the pain of loss is invisible.

Invisible pain often carries with it embarrassment, hopelessness, guilt, and shame. That is because the enemy wants to use your loss to bring shame and reproach upon you. Do not take the bait and embrace the enemy's shame and reproach. Trust and believe that God still has great plans for you.

Two things God makes known in Isaiah 66:9. First, God work is perfect. He will never abandon anything. All of his promises will be performed; all He has spoken concerning you will be accomplished. Second, Our God is so mighty and awesome; He can bring life out of our pain. But your breakthrough comes through prayer.

Perhaps you feel you have suffered loss alone. Perhaps it was not the loss of a child but the loss of a vision God placed in you. Instead of coming full-term, it lay still and lifeless in your womb. Communicate your confusion and frustration to the Father. Amazingly, when you talk to Him, you can say what you want to say. Lay it all out before Him.

Imagine the things that would change and be transformed in your life if you could just say what you want to say to the almighty God. Imagine what would happen if you not only said those things but then also took the time to hear what He is saying to you. God is a God of deliverance and restoration. Every mother who shares her experience of labor tells a different story, and your personal story of deliverance will be just as unique.

God will not abandon you, and He never wastes a hurt. What if this path, the one marked with pain, was the one God intended for you to take? The Bible says, "He knows the pathway that I take; if he tested me, I would come forth like gold" (Job 20:10, NET).

Edwin Louis Cole, an author and founder of the Christian Men's Network, once said, "God never ends anything on a negative; God always ends on a positive."[2]

Chapter 16
No Longer Sad

A joyful heart makes a cheerful face, but when the heart is sad, the spirit is broken.

—PROVERBS 15:13, NASB

I know firsthand what it's like to struggle with the anxiety of depression. For eight long years, I lived with what is known as SAD (Seasonal Affective Disorder). It is a type of depression related to changes in seasons. It begins and ends at about the same time every year, usually during a change of seasons or when an occasion that evokes painful memories is approaching, such as an anniversary, birthday, or the holidays.

Like most people with SAD, I camouflaged my problem through isolation. Since several holidays are on Mondays, I had to withdraw for only one day. I would confine myself to my apartment and hibernate. I would sleep the day away and anxiously await the next morning when I could return to work, where everything in the world would appear normal again.

However, every year, like clockwork, the approaching holidays would trigger my disorder. Thanksgiving and

Christmas were the hardest. These times when families gather to share and celebrate became my certain enemy. I spent three, sometimes four, days shrouded in gloom and heartache.

I despised the shopping, the cooking, the decorating, and the gift wrapping. At every invitation, I would try hard to accommodate family with my presence. Nevertheless, at best, the visit would become a battle of wills between my siblings and me. After a while, I would ignore their phone calls altogether and show up near the end of the day.

Through all of this, my family never stopped trying to reach out to me. They named me Scrooge. I was misunderstood and misdiagnosed, but my family never associated my mood change with depression. Church folk never knew, and even my friends, as they celebrated each holiday with great excitement, were oblivious to my condition.

The hardest thing about what I was dealing with was that people didn't understand my plight. They would chalk it up as me being difficult, mean, or antisocial. In truth, I was in real pain, a pain I could not verbalize. My spirit had been crushed and broken to the point of hopelessness. I would be driven to tears if I tried to explain it, but the Lord would remind me of Psalm 34:18, "The Lord is close to the brokenhearted and saves those who are crushed in spirit" (NIV).

There can be many reasons why we are left with a broken heart and sad: the death of a loved one, divorce, loss of a job, loss of status, loss of health, betrayal by a friend, loss of a child and, yes, loss of your childhood. All of these reasons can leave you a broken man or woman. You are left with this huge gaping hole in your heart that was left by someone or circumstances. After a while you may feel as though this hole can never be filled and that you will be left with the hollow in your heart forever. Psalm 147:3, says "He heals the brokenhearted and binds up their wounds" (NIV). God is the source of emotional healing. However, every Believer must pursue God daily for healing to take place.

Sometimes you have to pray with a broken heart. That's what Hannah did.

Praying with a broken heart is difficult but not impossible. The apostle Paul tells us in Romans 8:26 that when our mouths cannot utter the words, then our spirit will speak for us. Such is the story of Hannah in 1 Samuel 1:9–19, who sought the Lord with tears to have a child.

> *After they had eaten and drunk in Shiloh, Hannah rose. Now Eli the priest was sitting on the seat beside the doorpost of the temple of the LORD. She was deeply distressed and prayed to the LORD and wept bitterly.*
>
> —1 SAMUEL 1:9–10, ESV

Even though she desperately wanted to have a child for her husband, Hannah was barren. Like so many, Hannah tried to walk through her pain by herself. But at the same time every year when it was time to go to festival,

Hannah experienced a deep sadness. She isolated herself while everyone else was taking part in the festivities.

The Bible says she went to the temple along with her family for the annual festival, but instead of joining in the festivities, Hannah went to the temple to pray. As she lay prostrate before the Lord, Hannah was so engulfed in prayer that she did not notice when the priest Eli walked in. The Bible says her mouth was moving, but no words or sounds were coming out of her mouth—that's how intensely she was praying.

As the story continues, when Eli the priest approached her, he initially thought she was crazy—drunk even—from the feast. He asked her, "Woman, how long will you be drunken?" Hannah responded by telling him, "I'm not drunk. Don't count me as a worthless woman." Then she began to share her plight with him.

> [16] Do not take your servant for a wicked woman; I have been praying here out of my great anguish and grief." 17 Eli answered, "Go in peace, and may the God of Israel grant you what you have asked of him." 18 She said, "May your servant find favor in your eyes." Then she went her way and ate something, and her face was no longer downcast.
>
> —1 SAMUEL 1:16–18, NIV

A Good Word. Eli, the priest speaks a word of hope into Hannah's life.

We read in Proverbs 12:25, Anxiety in a man's heart weighs it down [depression], but a good word cheers it up." (HCSB). The word translated "good" in Proverbs 12:25 (or "kind" in the King James Version) is the Hebrew word *tov*. Perhaps you have heard it used in phrase "*Mazel tov* (good destiny)." *Mazal or mazel,* is the Hebrew word for destiny. *Tov* can mean good, beautiful, proper, right, jubilant, gracious, or festive (a cause to celebrate).

I imagine that the entire time Hannah was speaking, she was sobbing and inconsolable. At that point, Eli comforted her and reassured her that what she asked the Lord for that day, He would grant her. He told her to go in peace, and Hannah suddenly felt comforted.

God not only comforted her; He gave her the desire of her heart. He will do the same for you. The pain you feel is real and it may seem that you'll never find a way out, but we serve the God of all comfort. If you will turn to Him in prayer as Hannah did, He will comfort you and remove your sadness.

We may be able to relate to her desperation, but there is a difference between Hannah and us. In her day, the people needed an earthly priest to go to God on their behalf. Although that priest would present their concerns to God, he could only sympathize with their problems.

That is not the case with us. We know according to Hebrews 4:15 that, "We do not have a high priest who is unable to empathize with our weaknesses" (ESV). In other words, we do not have a high priest who is just going to God on our behalf. We have one who enters the throne room with us, covering us with His blood and making it possible for us to receive a good or kind word directly from the throne of God.

If I can highlight one thing that captured my heart about Hannah's story, it would be found in 1 Samuel 1:18: "And she said, 'Let your servant find favor in your eyes" (ESV). Having already made her petition known and having already made a vow before the Lord, Hannah prepared to leave the temple but not before ensuring the priest would take her request to the Father on her behalf. After that, the Bible says, Hannah got up, went to the festival, and ate. The last portion of verse 18 says, "…and her face was no longer sad."

A broken heart causes despondency and despair. The thing about sadness is that though it occurs in your heart, it will affect your outward man as well. So what did Hannah look like? Did she look like a hag? Did she not care about what she wore or how her hair was styled? Was she wearing makeup, or was she plain and somber? I am not sure what Hannah looked like when she was in the temple, but one thing for sure is the woman who went in the temple that day was not the same woman who came out. Hannah's entire demeanor had changed. Prayer and a word changed Hannah. It changed her outlook. It gave her hope and a future.

When Eli spoke a good word into Hannah's life, he may not have resolved her problem, but he caused her countenance to change and some of her burden to be relieved. Her situation had not yet changed, but change had taken place inside of her.

Like Hannah, when I was in despair, I had to lay it all out before the Lord—the good, the bad, and the ugly. Even when I prayed, my SAD did not disappear all at once. But every day, it got better and I was less sad. I received my healing as I determined to face each day knowing that my greatest resource for healing was prayer and God's Word.

One word from the Lord can change everything. Aligning your thought life with the Word of God is the key to an elevated life.

People who seek help for depression usually go to therapy sessions where they talk with others who have the same struggles. Sometimes just sharing our struggles with fellow-strugglers is helpful. But is it lasting, and does this alone bring healing? Sadness and anxiety in our hearts weighs us down. "But a good word makes it glad." Prov. 12:25 is talking about a good word from outside. A good word that makes the heart of the depressed glad has to be a word from God.

Of course, some types of depression require both prayer and clinical assistance. Depression is often an inner turmoil in which your mind is filled with many thoughts and fears, and it can manifest itself in extreme sadness. God uses many sources to bring about healing in our lives—including clinical assistance and medication. Please know there is nothing wrong with seeking professional help. Sometimes God wants to use Christian medical professionals to help you in your healing process.

If you feel a little down as the seasons change, you are not alone. Even if you are walking in your deliverance, SAD has a way of sneaking back up on you. I cannot emphasize it enough—*pray*. In everything you do, always consider the greatest resource we have. Pray about everything. God cares for you. What you are so concerned with isn't bigger than your God, so go to Him in prayer.

Along with prayer, I encourage you to try these practical steps to change your day:

>   Get outside.
>   Work out.
>   Stay social.
>   Read your Word.

The good word Proverbs 12:25 speaks of may not resolve whatever problem you may have, but it will cheer you up. 'Being cheerful keeps you healthy..." (Prov. 17:22a GNT)

Part IV
Vertical View in Perceived Failure

Life's challenges are not supposed to paralyze you: they're supposed to help you discover who you are.

-Bernice Johnson Reagon

Chapter 17
More Than Able

By this power he can do infinitely more than we can ask or imagine.

—EPHESIANS 3:20, GWT

What would you ask God for if you were absolutely confident He was listening?

Imagine with me the scene at Mount Carmel documented in 1 Kings 18. The prophet Elijah is in a showdown with 450 prophets of Baal. Aiming to prove whose god was real, Elijah called for two bulls to be placed on the altar. The prophets of Baal would call out to their god, and Elijah would call out to the God of Israel. The one who answered would be recognized as the only true God.

Baal was an ancient Near Eastern god that had long been worshipped in the region. The people put their trust in him, gave their money in his temples, and prayed and made sacrifices to him. If he wasn't real, they had been wasting their time. So the 450 prophets spend all day and night crying out to Baal to send fire from heaven and burn up the offering on the altar. They jumped through all kinds of hoops to get Baal to answer them, even stomping and cutting themselves to get their god to respond. But Baal couldn't answer them.

Then in a simple move, Elijah stepped forward to prove who the one true God really was. He rebuilt the altar and prepared a sacrifice. The Bible goes into great detail about how the altar was arranged. This is significant because the altar was set up differently from every other altar mentioned in Scripture before that point. The text says stones were arranged to form the altar. Next, a ditch was dug around the altar. Then wood was put in place. After that, the bull was cut into pieces and laid on top of the wood. Finally, once the altar was prepared, Elijah asked those who were assisting him to take four large jugs of water and drench the sacrifice and the altar with them three times. Seems a little crazy, doesn't it?

Just imagine if you were getting ready for a barbecue and after you set up the grill and added the coals and the accelerant, someone comes along and pours water all over your coals. It would be nearly impossible to start a fire, wouldn't it? Yet that's exactly what Elijah did, and in doing so he created an impossible situation. Now it would take an extraordinary, supernatural act to ignite this sacrifice. With this nearly impossible scenario, there would be only one entity who could step in and answer.

But Elijah wasn't intimidated. We know that because of the way he called out to God. He simply asked God to show Himself strong.

> *Lord, the God of Abraham, Isaac and Israel, let it be known today that you are God in Israel and that I am your servant and have done all these things at your command. Answer me, LORD, answer me, so these people will know that you, LORD, are God.*
>
> —1 KINGS 18:36–37, NIV

While Elijah was still praying, fire rained down from heaven. The Bible is very specific about what happened next. It says in verse 38 that the fire burned up the sacrifice, the wood, the stones, and the dirt, and licked up all the water. Now that was some fire!

The reason we do not see the impossible happen in our lives is that we pray only for the possible. We ask only for what we have already seen. We expect only what has already been. As it was with Elijah, when we pray we can be assured that God will not only show up, but He will demonstrate what He is able to do. Without a doubt, God can take an impossible situation and not just turn it around, but turn it around in a marked way. He will do it so that everyone watching will know that only God could have done this thing.

What a big God! What a mighty God He is! As Bible teacher A. W. Tozer once said, "Anything God has ever done, he can do now. Anything God has ever done anywhere, he can do here. Anything God has ever done for anyone, he can do for you."[1]

I know I have some impossible situations in my life today, some very real circumstances that I need God to answer. Perhaps you or someone you know is facing something right now that, it seems, will never be resolved. It is time for a supernatural move of God. Ephesians 3:20 says, "By this power he can do infinitely more than we can ask or imagine" (GWT).

God can do infinitely more than we realize. He can solve our every problem—it does not matter whether it is a circumstance we just cannot seem to resolve or a hardship that is entirely out of our control. Instead of asking simply for money to pay the bills, why not ask God to give you a plan to eliminate your debt? You did not come this far to walk away without the victory. Pray and be confident that God is more than able.

Chapter 18
I Can Fix It!

> *Praying is what confirms our true belief that we cannot succeed without God—and its absence confirms the exact opposite.[1]*
>
> —JAMES MACDONALD

If you have ever been around a toddler with a broken toy, then you have heard these words before: *I can fix it!* Our children learn these four words of self-efficacy at a very early age. Self-efficacy is the extent or strength of one's belief in one's own ability to complete tasks and reach goals. Children are aware that you are daddy or mommy, but in their struggle for independence, they refuse to rely on your assistance to accomplish any task. Doing things themselves makes them feel BIG. They spend countless minutes trying to force pieces together that do not fit. Then finally, they succumb to tears and frustration and acknowledge they really do need your help.

Just as children are learning to rely on their own perceived ability, many of us have been conditioned to make decisions and respond to problems through our own efforts. The result is we make circumstances worse by trying to solve them through our reasoning or our natural skills. What we should do is seek God for the answer and wait for Him to impact the problem.

God knows the solution to the problem before it ever exists. Our responsibility is to ask God for help solving the problem and rely on Him for the outcome. The minute we take matters into our own hands, just like a toddler does, God quietly stands by to let us experience failure until we decide to let go.

Proverbs 16:3 tells us to commit our works to God so our plans will be established. In the original Hebrew, the word translated "commit" means to "roll over."[1] The Classic Edition of the Amplified Bible puts it this way: "Roll your works upon the Lord [commit and trust them wholly to Him; He will cause your thoughts to become agreeable to His will, and] so shall your plans be established and succeed."

The wording in this translation creates the picture of a camel laden with a lot of stuff. The camel is an interesting animal. It is not one of the most beautiful creatures. It has thick, matted hair that falls off in clumps. It has knobby knees and a big hump on its back. It is referred to as a ruminant, because much like a cow, it regurgitates its swallowed food to chew again, and then swallows it again. However, the camel is a wonderful animal when you need to carry a lot of stuff. Used for transportation in many countries, camels can carry up to six hundred pounds and average twenty miles a day over rugged terrain. They can travel in hot conditions and go for long periods of time without water. They truly are amazing animals.

Each night at the end of a long day, when it was time to unload the packs, the camel would kneel at the feet of its master. The master would then have the camel lie down on the ground, and the camel would roll the load off. The owner would carefully remove the burden from the camel so it could rest comfortably through the night. The next morning, the camel would again kneel before its master, and the master would gently place the burden back on the camel for another day's journey. The master would be careful to rearrange things here or there if he saw that the pack was wearing a sore spot so the camel would be able to continue carrying its load.

What a powerful analogy. Your works, your responsibilities are sometimes like a heavy burden you carry on your back with no clue of how to get it off. If you take your lead from the camel, you might find that the best, and probably only, solution to get a heavy burden off your back is to dump it at the Lord's feet and ask Him to take charge of it.

Kneel at the feet of the Master. Articulate your concerns through prayer. Tell Him, "Lord, I'm not quite sure how it will work out, but I'm committing it to You. I'm putting it into Your hands." Then let Him take charge of it. He will relieve the pressures of your day.

You can commit it to Him! When I purchased my first car, my stepfather taught me how to change a tire. That knowledge really came in handy. It felt great to know how to handle a tire and jack all on my own. When I got married, I did not forget how to change a tire. I just figured I didn't need to work that hard at something not designed for me to do. My husband was much stronger than I was and built for the task. That didn't take anything away from me. I just decided to roll the task over onto him.

We all have our own plans, our own agendas, and the desire to do things our own way. Actually, we make our way hard when we do not seek His help. You may want to do it all by yourself, but you really do need the Father's help. The Father is asking us to carry only the loads that He has equipped and prepared us to carry. Roll every care, concern, and responsibility off your back. Once you do, God can establish and direct you. At the end of the day, it is the end of the day. Cast. Roll. Commit. As Calvary Chapel pastor Chuck Smith once said, "Commit your best and the Lord will do the rest."[3]

Chapter 19
The Finished Product

The LORD will perfect that which concerneth me.

—PSALM 138:8, KJV

The Facebook post by a friend simply read, "Perfection is the enemy of greatness." Then I thought to myself, "Isn't that what we all strive for?" We strive to procure the perfect job, the perfect mate, the perfect house. When we have a special affair to attend, we want the perfect little black dress or suit and accessories to match. After we get dressed, we look in the mirror and say to ourselves, "Perfect!" Yet a closer look at the meaning of this empowering word will also reveal its ability to impede even the most confident individual's progress.

Being perfect would imply that you have reached perfection. Someone who is a perfectionist is striving to be perfect, and that implies that he or she isn't there yet. According to Merriam-Webster's dictionary, *perfect* means to be *entirely without fault or defect*.[1] That definition has incapacitated even the most gifted people. Anyone striving for perfection has a high bar to reach. The dictionary tells us that perfection is "the quality or state of being perfect...freedom from fault or defect."[2]

All true believers know perfection is a process God takes us through. The apostle Paul wrote in Philippians 3:12, "I do not claim that I have already succeeded or have already become perfect. I keep striving to win the prize for which Christ Jesus has already won me to himself" (GNT). In other words, Paul was saying he was not perfect, even though perfection was his goal.

In Matthew 5:48 when Jesus spoke about having love for others, He used the term "perfect," a word that can also be translated to mean "holy."[3] Jesus said, "Therefore you are to be perfect, as your heavenly Father is perfect" (NASB). In this particular text, the word *perfect* means having all of the required or desirable elements, qualities, or characteristics; lacking nothing. This verse is telling us that the Father makes us perfect. He perfects us.

I consider myself the world's greatest procrastinator. Sometimes it works to my advantage; other times, not so much. However, behind my procrastination lies the need to be perfect. I tried for a very long time to put something into print that would be a blessing to others. I have started and stopped several books.

Whenever I stopped, it was often because I would notice the imperfections in my work. I'd wonder how I ever could have thought I was as capable as others with similar callings. I'd tell myself that my speaking and writing were just not on their level. I'd worry about people criticizing my work. Overwhelmed by the belief that whatever I did would fail, I became convinced that I should not even try to put anything out.

My experience is a common one. Many people fear completing a task or assignment. Sometimes they are unsure of what to do so they never begin; sometimes they become so distracted they never complete it. Some dare to blame the delay on their personality—"Oh, the reason I haven't finished yet is because I'm a perfectionist." However, it is usually the fear of judgment or rejection that is really holding them back. *Don't buy into the perfectionist lie.*

One day while doing research for a project, I came across a book titled *When Your Best Is Good Enough* by Dr. Kevin Leman. In his book, Dr. Leman writes, "Perfection is slow suicide. … Perfectionists organize by piles. They do not finish projects. They wrongly believe that someday they will be perfect, so they don't even start."[4]

Hmm. Does that sound like anyone you know, besides me? The bottom line is this—the pursuit of perfection is frustrating, neurotic, and a terrible waste of time. I quickly realized that it was not my attempts to have a perfect product but my struggle to be perfect that derailed me from finishing every book project. What I should have been striving for was godly excellence in whatever I attempted. Striving for excellence means you do your best and are content to leave the rest to God.

In Psalm 138, David pauses in his difficulties and gives God praise for answering his prayers. He says, "When I called, you answered me" (verse 3, NIV). Throughout the psalm, David acknowledges his inability to accomplish anything outside the will of the Father. Then by the eighth verse, he discloses his confidence in God's ability to perfect (complete) everything that concerned his life.

This is our clue that we should praise God in advance for answered prayers. Even when we don't see the answers we seek, we must let the enemy know that we know God will perfect everything that concerns us. Adam Clarke's Bible commentary says it best, "Whatever is further necessary to be done, He will do it."[5] He will do it even in perceived failures because you are God's finished product.

Perhaps you have heard God leading you to take a step of faith toward something specific in your life. Obey His voice and don't forget to:

- Stay close to His Word.
- Get to know Him and His plans for you.
- Give yourself permission to be imperfect.
- Praise Him for answered prayers.

God will not begin a thing and not finish it. You may not have perfect pitch or the smoothest vocal ability. You may not have such a command of the English language that it will astound readers. Do what God is leading you to do anyway. Trust and know that somewhere in the earth somebody's life is waiting to be blessed by what you have to offer. *Nothing is perfected until it is completed*

Part V
Vertical View in Chaos and Crisis

Seeds of Faith are always within us; sometimes it takes a crisis to nourish and encourage growth.

—Susan Taylor

Chapter 20
I Know You Weren't Prepared for This!

From the end of the earth will I cry unto thee, when my heart is overwhelmed: lead me to the rock that is higher than I.

—PSALM 61:2, KJV

I am sure you have seen or heard the Nationwide Insurance commercials that end with the slogan, "Life comes at you fast." They're simply saying trouble, catastrophes, and bad things usually come at you when you least expect them. On top of that, sometimes no matter how prepared you are, life hands you experiences that, in your mind, just were not supposed to happen.

My husband began to complain of nagging chest pains and trouble breathing. Having lost his biological father at an early age to a heart disease, he thought he might experience the same fate. Every day I would ask what was bothering him, but he would say, "Nothing." Then finally one morning, unable to conceal his condition, he decided to tell me that along with the pain, he was throwing up blood.

We immediately scheduled an appointment with his general practitioner, who sent him to a gastroenterology specialist. Following an exam and consultation, the specialist said my husband's test showed he had a case of extreme anemia. Right away, he scheduled a procedure that would allow them to take a closer look at his esophagus and stomach and better determine the cause of his pain and loss of blood. However, being a pastor, my husband was more concerned about getting back to church for Bible study than having the procedure done. Therefore, he delayed it.

When the day finally arrived for his procedure, we traveled over an hour from our home to the specialist's office. The doctor told us the procedure would take approximately one hour, including recovery time. However, fifteen minutes later, just as I sat down to read a magazine, the nurse called me back to the recovery area. The doctor looked concerned and showed me a gruesome picture of a bleeding gastric ulcer about the size of a golf ball. Then, following a brief consultation, I was told they would be admitting my husband to the hospital. Because of the bleeding, I would not be allowed to take him home or transport him myself. He would need to be transported by ambulance.

A word in due season...how sweet it is. (See Proverbs 15:23.)

There is power in a right word. Immediately, I called the children to inform them that their dad was about to be admitted to the hospital for the very first time in his life. Though the concern was for their dad, our daughter asked, "Is there anything you need?" Before I could respond, she said to me, "I know you weren't prepared for this." There was nothing truer. It never crossed any of our minds that a routine procedure would turn into a life-altering moment for us all. It was too much. The day was not supposed to go in that direction.

My heart was overwhelmed. I am not sure if my daughter realized then that God was using her at that very moment to speak prophetically into my life. With those right-now words came a reminder that this battle was spiritual, and it required the use of spiritual lenses to understand what God was doing.

Even when we are facing overwhelming challenges, God will speak a right-now word that not only reminds us that people care, but that He cares for us. The right word at the wrong moment can cause confusion, but the right word at the right time has the power to lift your weariness and change your view of the circumstance. The prophet Isaiah said, "The Lord GOD hath given me the tongue of the learned, that I should know how to speak a word in season to him that is weary" (Is. 50:4, KJV). Another translation says it this way, "The Lord God has given Me the tongue of a disciple and of one who is taught, that I should know how to speak a word in season to him who is weary" (AMPC).

There is nothing like having a word in season when you're going through a trial to help alter your perspective. In Psalm 61 when David was faced with a tremendous challenge, his heart was overwhelmed. So he asked the Lord to change his vantage point, to take him to the Rock that was higher than his finite mind or comprehension.

By doing this, he was asking the Lord to help him see his situation from the Father's perspective.

Perspective has a Latin root meaning to look through or perceive, and all the meanings of perspective have something to do with looking. Perspective has everything to do with how you view things. When I see a situation from God's perspective, I am able to see it accurately instead of from a limited human standpoint. Instead I see the problem in light of God's ability. Thus, when we see things from God's point of view, we can face difficulties with confidence.

I have several friends who are going through some very difficult times in their lives. Some are experiencing downsizing on their jobs. Some had loved ones pass away from cancer or another disease. Some have marriages that are broken, seemingly beyond repair, while others have various health challenges. They feel they are facing these life difficulties alone. As a result, they are trying to work things out by themselves. The one thing that can make people quit is when they feel they have been left all alone.

Some of us spend more time working things out for ourselves than seeking the face of God, or we spend more time listening to others than listening to the voice of God. A shift in our perspective can calm our hearts about some of the things that worry us—if we can see our challenges, not from our perspective but from God's perspective.

A perspective shift helps you face another day.

Life will blindside you, and though you may not think you're prepared for the challenge in the natural, the Father already knew what you were going to face when you woke up that day. The truth is, you cannot control what happens to you, but you can choose what happens in you. Every significant crisis in your life can be a turning point. What we see or hear does not tell us everything we know. When you face life's difficult moments, do not look at them from your limited, fearful, unsure point of view. See them from God's powerful, unlimited, heightened, greater point of view. See them from a heavenly perspective. Perhaps you are being called to endure this crisis for a higher purpose. Learn to lean on God and His faithfulness.

Remind yourself that the Father will meet every need and He will never leave you. Then confidently place your future in His Hands, for He cares. Today ask the Father to help you think not from your own earthly perspective, but from His heavenly perspective. It helps when you can change your vantage point to one that requires total trust in His providence. Rest assured, God will come through for you.

Seeing the hand of God in your situation may seem impossible when the bottom drops out from your life, but viewing life from a vertical perspective gives you hope and helps you stand firm. No matter what the crisis. Pray with your eyes on God, not on your difficulties.

Today, my husband stands stronger in his faith than ever before. He walks in total healing with no signs that the illness ever existed in his body!

Chapter 21
Before You Go to Pieces

Worry does not empty tomorrow of its sorrow.
It empties today of its strength.

—CORRIE TEN BOOM

"I can't breathe…I need you to pray for me," uttered a distressed young woman from the other end of the phone.

"Can you tell me what happened?" I asked.

As I listened to her struggle to get the words out through her sobs and tears, it became apparent that whatever she had just encountered was now triggering a panic attack. She was a babe in Christ, so it was important for her to know that I was genuinely concerned for her.

"Where are you?" I asked.

"In my car," she replied.

I instructed her to pull her car off the main street into a safe, well-lit area. Once I was able to assess that she was in no immediate danger, I began sharing with her a simple relaxation technique that would help reduce her anxiety level.

"Take slow, deep, even breaths," I said. "That will help you breathe easier."

The technique is great because it is the same way newborn babies naturally breathe.

"Inhale slowly and deeply through your nose," I said. "Relax. Exhale slowly through your mouth. Now tell me your story."

When she had finished speaking, we prayed. After our prayer, I instructed her to turn her radio to the gospel station, or if she had any worship CDs in her car to select a song that ministers to her. Then I had her start her car and come to the church where a Bible study was in progress. Later that evening, there was a text to my phone that simply read, "Just wanted to say thanks and I love you… (Smile emoji)"

All of us have faced anxiety at times in our lives. Anxiety is merely a form of worry or fear, usually based on circumstances we have no control over. Just about every situation in life has the potential to cause you to worry or become anxious. Anxiety paired with worry and fear of the unknown can often cause pain or "panic."

In this young woman's case, she became overwhelmed with anxiety when a simple parent conference went spiraling out of control.

> *Do not worry. Learn to pray about everything. Give thanks to God as you ask Him for what you need.*
>
> —PHILIPPIANS 4:6, NLV

In Philippians 4:6, Paul comes to the rescue of the church at Philippi during a time when the gospel brought persecution. He reminded them of the need to remain calm in every situation, not allowing their present condition or the threat of future events to cause them anxiety or panic. The word translated anxious in this verse has its root in the Greek word *merimnao*, which means to be pulled in different directions, or more literally "to go to pieces."[1]

Can you picture the church at Philippi? Their lives were so full of turmoil that it caused them to literally lose it and go to pieces. Imagine yourself coming to the Lord with a heavy burden, something you know you cannot handle on your own. No matter how hard you try, it is weighing you down. Logically you should worry, and people are even telling you that you should be anxious.

One can understand why we sometimes go to pieces. There are times when our hopes pull us in one direction and our fears pull us in the opposite direction. We may even feel like our minds cannot take much more. Of course, the Word has something to say about that: Worry about nothing. Pray about everything!

Only when we invite God into our fears will our anxiety disappear. I am not suggesting that we simply act carefree. I am suggesting that we give the burden or care totally to the Father, knowing that only He can take it away. Remember:

- **Before you panic, pray.** Tell the Father exactly what you are dealing with. He already knows, but telling Him releases Him to act on your behalf.

- **While you pray, give up control.** God will not do for you what you insist on doing yourself. Trust that He can handle the situation much better than you can.

- **After you pray, release it with thanksgiving.** Give Him the praise in advance, and walk away in perfect peace, with no worries!

Chapter 22: Hunker Down

Sometimes you just have to bow your head, say a prayer, and weather the storm!

— DEBORAH WHITE

If you live anywhere in the South, you have probably heard or even used the term "hunker down." News reporters use it to warn residents to make preparation for an approaching storm. The phrase typically means "to dig in or crouch for the purpose of waiting out or avoiding an undesirable event or situation."[1] However, hunker down is actually a hunting term. During hunting season, deer find shelter, crouch down, and hold their position until the threat passes, making it difficult for hunters to find them.

I received a prayer request via e-mail. Concerned, I replied by asking if she was having a rough day. Her answer was, "Yeah. Overwhelmed, confused. I am trying to stay focused, but it is difficult some days and today is one of them… I'll be glad when this HURRICANE is over."

I did not send a second reply immediately because I needed time to meditate on the word she capitalized: HURRICANE. What she wanted me to know is that she was not experiencing a regular rainstorm. A hurricane is a storm, but as it moves across the ocean, it builds strength and speed. She was in the midst of a storm, and it had developed into something more catastrophic—a hurricane.

Searching for a reference point, I started thinking back to an actual hurricane. Of course, Hurricane Katrina came to mind. In terms of devastation, Katrina was one of the costliest natural disasters and one of the deadliest hurricanes in the history of this country. Nearly 2,000 people lost their lives in the actual hurricane and in the subsequent floods, and hundreds of thousands were displaced from their homes. The damage was in the billions of dollars.[2] Afterward, many questioned the very existence of God while others prophesied that it was a sign of the end times.

The year after Katrina hit, I was traveling with a group of women to Houston, Texas, for a convention. As we approached Louisiana, we decided to drive into the city of New Orleans to get a closer look at the storm's aftermath. As we drove slowly through the streets, my heart sank at the scene one year later. Though we had not been in the storm or affected directly by it, the sight overwhelmed us.

Tears welled up in my eyes. I could almost hear the people scream as they ran for their lives, trying desperately to save themselves and others, only to realize that they could not save everyone. We were looking at what remained after the water rescinded. Before us were decay, destruction, and devastation. It was like a scene from the movie *Deep Impact*, in which two comets were on a course to collide with Earth. After all the fear, death, and devastation, the lives of those survivors in Louisiana would never be the same.

I wondered if this was equivalent to my friend's storm. All of us go through storms in life. If we haven't just come out of a storm, we are either in the midst of a storm or will be facing a storm in the coming days. Not all storms can be associated with rain and fierce wind. There are situations you can encounter in life that will put everything in your life into a different focus. You begin to wonder if you are going to make it through the storm. Those around you wonder how you are going to cope with the storm. You cannot see how you are going to work things out.

Your storm might be loss, death, depression, disappointment, divorce, or rejection. When you're in a storm, often there does not really seem to be any explanation for what you're going through, and you are not sure you really understand what is going on. However, just before you break, just when you think you are about to go under, God will send someone to strengthen you.

Sometimes, the storm is necessary. The prophet Isaiah wrote, "It will be a shelter and shade from the heat of the day, and a refuge and hiding place from the storm and rain" (Is. 4:6, NIV, emphasis added).

Your storm is not random. God anticipated it. Every now and then, you will go through something you cannot control the outcome of, that money cannot buy your way out of, and that education cannot secure, and you will have to look to the Father for help. You may feel that God has abandoned you or that He is not there and not listening to your prayer. But that is not true. God is faithful to His believers.

Lean on the Word of God. Know that until the storm passes, God promises to provide every possible protection imaginable. Cry out to Him, asking not that He would conform His will to yours, but that you would surrender to His.

He knows your name. He knows your struggle. Ask Him to walk you through it. He may not take away the rain, but He will protect you from its impact. You will not be utterly destroyed. Hunker down in the arms of the Father, and He will see you through the storm.

Part VI
Vertical Lifeline

If you only pray when you're in trouble, you're in trouble.

-Author Unknown

Chapter 23
Pray First

We tend to use prayer as a last resort, but God wants it to be our first line of defense.

—OSWALD CHAMBERS

Prayer is not just an exercise, but it is a function of a relationship. However, most of us do what is termed "crisis praying." We pray only in moments of trial and testing. The danger in crises is easy to see; we find ourselves fearful, making major life-changing decisions, and managing serious risks. However, right alongside the danger in the crisis lies something not always so easy to see: an opportunity to grow through the trial or to discover God's purpose for our lives.

We have all had our periods, seasons, or events of "crisis." Every crisis is an opportunity for God to bring about transformation (change). God uses crises to teach us important things. A crisis can reveal things to us we never would have known had the crisis not occurred.

Ultimately, God has a way—whether it's locusts destroying crops in Joel's time (Joel 2:25) or the bottom falling out of the economy in ours—of using crisis as an opportunity to shape our future and help us grow stronger and more mature in faith. As author E. M. Bounds wrote, "Prayer should not be regarded as a duty, which must be performed, but rather as a privilege to be enjoyed."[1]

Our crisis can lead us to pray. While most people do not pray until there is a problem, our prayers should not be driven by a need or a crisis. How would you feel if a person sent an invitation or visited only when they needed something from you? The Father knows we will pray in times of need and crisis, but can He count on us to show up when there is not one?

In other words, we pray if there is nothing else we can do. However, God wants us to pray before we do anything at all. Let us learn from Jesus's example. The Bible says, "Very early in the morning, while it was still dark, Jesus got up, left the house and went off to a solitary place, where he prayed" (Mark 1:35, NIV).

I once heard Pastor Chris Hodges of the Church of the Highlands teach a lesson about praying first. In his message, he made these three observations from Mark 1:35:

1. Jesus had a time, a place, and a plan for prayer.

2. Jesus got up very early in the morning to spend time with His heavenly Father.

3. Jesus prayed consistently, continually, and confidently

Prayer is your first line of defense. For many of us, our tendency is to exhaust every avenue before we seek God. Then when nothing else works, we seek Him to bail us out of the situation. The Father is not a bail bondsman. Prayer should always be our first response, not our last. We should pray:

- Before the day begins

- Before we eat, drive, or travel

- Before we go to work or school

- Before we apply for that job or loan

- Before we go on that interview

- Before we send that text or post that tweet

- When bad things happen

- Before bad things happen

In every situation, whether good or bad, try to pray before you act. First Thessalonians 5:16–18 tells us to "rejoice always, pray continually, give thanks in all circumstances; for this is God's will for you in Christ Jesus" (NIV).

When you spend time in daily conversation with the Father, you will experience the presence of God that will change your life. When you find yourself in a time of crisis, you will always resort back to what you know to be sound and true—that accepting God's invitation to come to Him in prayer brings confidence, boldness, and hope like none other.

What are you waiting for? He has made the first move. Let us go to the Father today.

How to Seek God in Prayer

1. Accept the Father's invitation to seek Him (Luke 11:23, 24; Matt. 7:11; Ps. 65:2; Mark 11:23–24).

2. Bring to Him everything that troubles you or concerns you in any way (1 Pet. 5:7; Ps. 55:22).

3. Mingle praise, gratitude, and thanksgiving with all of your prayers (Phil. 1:4; Col. 3:15–17; 1 Thess. 5:18).

4. Pursue oneness with the mind of God and deep fellowship with Him, for that is the purpose of prayer (Rev. 3:20; Eph. 3:16–19).

5. Find a quiet place to pray and seek God each day with your whole heart (Mark 1:35; Jer. 29:13).

6. Use the power of your words combined with what God has written in His Word (Matt. 26:39; Luke 11:1).

7. Record God's answers in a prayer journal and read them periodically to remind yourself of His blessings (Deut. 8:2; 1 Chron. 16:12).

The key to having your prayers answered is this: Pray according to the will of God. You will know it's His will when what you pray is good and well-pleasing to God, and causes you to become mature and fully equipped to fulfill His purposes.

Appendix
Connect in Prayer

Rejoice and exult in hope; be steadfast and patient in suffering and tribulation; be constant in prayer.

—ROMANS 12:12, AMPC

The Bible is full of promises that you can pray for any circumstance in life. When you pray, it is important to pray what God says about your specific situation because "the Word of God is living and active and sharper than any two-edged sword," (Heb. 4:12, ESV). The spoken Word of God will produce power and life because that is the very nature of God. When you speak God's Word to Him and to situations, you release God's authority to bring blessing and change.

The prayers included in this section are only a sampling of prayers I have found to be effective in my life and in the lives of those I am praying for. They correspond with the themes in this book, and you may pray them anytime and anywhere. Pray these prayers as a weapon. Pray and things will start to happen. Speak a thing and the reality comes. Win the battle through prayer. Remember, as you pray you are shifting atmospheres.

PRAYER FOR LIFE CHALLENGES

Father, today I open my heart to You, to say yes to whatever You ask. I submit to Your will and ask that You be strong upon me. Lord, I am overwhelmed by the love You have for me, and I pray that You would allow me to know experientially how mighty You are to save, heal, and deliver. You are my strength and power, and You make my path plain. I know according to 2 Corinthians 4:8 that I am unbreakable and You have given me the power to overcome whatever challenges the world may throw my way. I settle to trust in You during the hard days and the difficult challenges that my journey may bring. My hope is in You. My trust is in You. My faith is in You. When I am weak, Your grace makes me strong. Thank You for that promise, in Jesus's name I pray. Amen.

PRAYER FOR GODLY COMMITMENT

Father, I want You at the center of my life. Today I commit through Your power to serve and obey You—anytime, anywhere, at any cost to do anything. I want to go where You lead. Give me a burden for prayer. I do not want a superficial prayer life, but the kind of prayer life that changes lives and the course of nations. Show me Your ways, LORD, teach me Your paths. Guide me in Your truth and teach me, for You are God my Savior, and my hope is in You all day long (Ps. 25:4–5). Lord, give me the courage to believe one more time. Give me the strength to see the invisible and reach for the impossible. Father, it is my heart's desire that You receive the glory in all that I do and say. In Jesus's name, amen.

PRAYER AGAINST DISTRACTIONS

Father, thank You for Your loving-kindness. Today, I need Your help to cut out the nonsense, the distractions, the obstacles, and the unnecessary events of the day. Help me to look past the things that appear good and seem important but only cause me to forget You. Quiet the noise in my mind. Help me to discipline myself to filter out the things that do not belong in my mind, my eyes, and my ears. I call my body, soul, and spirit into alignment with Your will and purpose. I acknowledge this day that Your grace is sufficient for every eventuality in my life. I have the mind of Christ. My feet walk in the paths You have ordained for me to walk. My steps are strong and steady. I make You my focus today, Father. In Jesus's name, I pray. Amen.

PRAYER AGAINST DISTRESS, GRIEF, AND LOSS

Father, it is not Your will that I carry my concerns alone. Thank You, Lord, for wanting me to only carry the loads You have equipped and prepared me to carry. I want to commit my ways, my plans, and my works to You, Father. Help me to commit every struggle, every disappointment, every heartache, and every work to Your care. Thank You for granting me the strength to make it through today as I cope with the sorrow and hurt of my circumstance. You have promised to carry our pain even when our hearts seem to fail. Father, I know that You are there to carry me and help me to move forward in life. I am determined to roll every care and concern over onto You, Lord. Thank You for giving me bright hope for tomorrow, for always being with me, and for the great comfort that I have in knowing You. In Jesus's name, I pray. Amen.

PRAYER IN THE MIDST OF PERCEIVED FAILURE

Lord, I am confident, knowing that according to Philippians 1:6, He who has begun a good work in me will complete it. I believe You, God, that You are going to address my concerns and complete Your absolutely perfect work in my life. I know that little becomes much when I place it in Your hand. Father, I want Your will to be my plans. I want Your glory to be my goal. I have things that I want to do.

But if these plans are not for Your glory, if these plans are not a blessing to my family or those over whom I have influence, then please guide me into areas of Your blessing. Thank You for bringing forth what You placed in me for the benefit of the body of Christ. Through Your gifts, may souls be saved, bodies healed, and the bound delivered. Father, equip me to do Your will. Work in me that which is well-pleasing in Your sight. Cause my delight to be in You. Let that be the greatest treasure of my heart. Align the desires of my heart with Yours, and may You receive all the glory. In Jesus's name, I pray. Amen.

PRAYER FOR TIMES OF CHAOS AND CRISIS (OR ANXIETY)

Father, I look to You as my source of hope and of peace. There is no need for me to stress or worry. You will provide everything I need for life, for peace, and for protection. Today I will not be anxious about anything, but I will pray to You about everything, casting my cares upon You because You care for me. You will guide me along the best pathway for my life. You will advise me and counsel me. There is no fear, no anxiety, and no panic in heaven. Lord God, help me to trust in You. Father, thank You for being here with me right now. Even in the chaos of my life, You will never leave me alone. You are always with me. At times, I feel overwhelmed, as if the world is closing in on me. Only You can bring order out of this chaos. You, the God of my life, are also the God of order. I surrender all the concerns that rise up around me like storm waves. Calm the seas and still the waters. Lord, may I rest in You, even in this day's most stressful moment. In Jesus's name, I pray. Amen.

Notes

Introduction

1. Beliefnet.com, Beliefnet's Inspirational Quotes, accessed September 24, 2016, *http://www.beliefnet.com/quotes/christian/o/oswald-chambers/prayer-does-not-fit-us-for-the-greater-work-praye.aspx.*

2. Christopher Crawford, as quoted by Christopher Sopko in *The Pyramid of Business Success* (New York: World's Best Business Books, 2014)

Chapter 2: A Confident Approach

1. Merriam-Webster's Learner's Dictionary s.v., "arrogance," accessed September 24, 2016, http://www.merriam-webster.com/dictionary/arrogance.

2. Dictionary.com, s.v., "confidence," accessed September 24, 2016, http://www.dictionary.com/browse/confidence?s=t.

3. Strong's Concordance, *"pístis,"* G4102, accessed September 24, 2016, http://biblehub.com/greek/4102.htm.

Chapter 3: Finding God's Frequency
1. Merriam-Webster.com, s.v., "white noise," accessed September 24, 2016, http://www.merriam-webster.com/dictionary/white%20noise.

2. Charles Stanley, *How to Listen to God* (Nashville, TN: Thomas Nelson, 1985). Viewed at Google Books.

Chapter 4: Exhaust Him
1. *Webster's Revised Unabridged Dictionary*, s.v., "exhaust," accessed September 24, 2016, http://biblehub.com/topical/e/exhaust.htm.

2. Max Lucado, "Trusting God When Your Future Is Up in the Air," Lifeway.com, accessed May 24, 2016, http://www.lifeway.com/Article/Max-Lucado-Grace-Trusting-God-When-Your-Future-is-Up-in-the-Air.

Chapter 5: Can Prayer Really Change Things?
1. John R. W. Stott, Romans: God's Good News for the World (Downers Grove, IL: InterVarsity, 1994), 389.

2. Rick Warren, "Your Life Is Shaped by Your Thoughts," RickWarren.org, June

www.rickwarren.org/listen-online/change-your-life-by-changing-your-mind-part-1/daily-radio.

Chapter 7: 24/7
1. E.M. Bounds, *Purpose in Prayer,* viewed at Christian Classics Ethereal Library, accessed June 8, 2016, http://www.ccel.org/ccel/bounds/purpose.II.html.

Chapter 10: Distractions
1. Kathleen Kulper, "Clyde Beatty," Encyclopaedia Britannica, September 2, 2015, accessed September 24, 2016, https://www.britannica.com/biography/Clyde-Beatty.

2. Ibid.

3. James Clear, "Lessons From a Lion Tamer: How to Focus and Concentrate Better," LewRockwell.com, March 27, 2013, accessed September 24, 2016, https://www.lewrockwell.com/2013/03/james-clear/lessons-from-a-lion-tamer/.

4. Ibid.

5. Ibid.

6. Merriam-Webster online, s.v., "divert," accessed September 25, 2016, http://www.merriam-webster.com/dictionary/divert.

Chapter 11: Waterfalls
1. Watchman Nee, Deep *Calls Unto Deep* (Anaheim, CA: Living Stream Ministry, 1998),

Chapter 12: Hitting the Wall!
1. Nicholas Huba, Sherlon Christie, and Ken Serrano, "Driver Dies After Crash at Racing Clinic in New Jersey," USA Today, August 17, 2014, accessed June 9, 2016, http://www.usatoday.com/story/sports/motor/2014/08/16/female-driver-dies-crash-wall-stadium-new-jersey-racing-clinic/14170383.

2. Bishop Dale Bronner tweet, shared by Bishop T.D. Jakes on April 23, 2016, accessed September 24, 2016, https://twitter.com/bishopjakes/status/723892838262562816.

Chapter 14: Lord, Keep My Mind!
1. Strong's Concordance, *"shalom,"* H7965, accessed September 25, 2016, https://www.blueletterbible.org/lang/lexicon/lexicon.cfm?t=kjv&strongs=h7965.

2. Corrie ten Boom's book The Hiding Place tells about how they hid Jews, were sent to a concentration camp, and led a Bible study and prayer meeting there. Some of the prisoners in that camp became Christians through their ministry.

3. Corrie ten Boom, Clippings from My Notebook (Nashville, Tennessee: Thomas Nelson Publishers, 1982), p. 27.

Chapter 15: A Message for Your Womb
1. March of Dimes, "Miscarriage," accessed June 7, 2016, http://www.marchofdimes.org/complications/miscarriage.aspx; Centers for Disease Control, "Facts About Stillbirth," accessed June 7, 2016, http://www.cdc.gov/ncbddd/stillbirth/facts.html.

2. Edwin Louis Cole, "Coleism," accessed June 7, 2016, https://www.edcole.org/index.php?fuseaction=coleisms.

Chapter 17: More Than Able
1. Preaching Today, "A. W. Tozer on God's Power," accessed June 8, 2016, http://www.preachingtoday.com/illustrations/2002/november/13958.html.

Chapter 18: I Can Fix It!
1. Twitter, @JamesMcDonald, December 19, 2015, accessed June 8, 2016, https://twitter.com/jamesmacdonald/status/678199379925176320.

2. Strong's Concordance, "galal," H1556, accessed September 25, 2016, https://www.blueletterbible.org/lang/Lexicon/Lexicon.cfm?strongs=H1556&t=KJV.

3. Chuck Smith, "Do Your Best, and Commit the Rest," Blue Letter Bible, accessed September 24, 2016, http://www.blbclassic.org/commentaries/comm_view.

Chapter 19: The Finished Product
1. Merriam-Webster's Learner's Dictionary, s.v., "perfect," accessed September 25, 2016, http://www.merriam-webster.com/dictionary/perfect.

2. Merriam-Webster's Learner's Dictionary, s.v., "perfection," http://www.merriam-webster.com/dictionary/perfection.

3. Strong's Concordance, "teleioō," G5048, https://www.blueletterbible.org/lang/Lexicon/Lexicon.cfm?strongs=G5048&t=KJV

4. Dr. Kevin Lemen, When Your Best Is Good Enough (Grand Rapids, MI: Revell, 2010).

5. Adam Clarke, The Holy Bible: Containing the Old and New Testaments ..., Volume 3 (New York: Abraham Paul, 1825), Psalm 138:3.

Chapter 21: Before You Go to Pieces
1. Strong's Concordance, "merimnao," G3309, accessed June 8, 2016, http://biblehub.com/greek/3309.htm.

Chapter 22: Hunker Down
1. Online Slang Dictionary, s.v.,hunker down," accessed June 8, 2016, http://onlineslangdictionary.com/meaning-definition-of/hunker-down.

2. History.com, "Hurricane Katrina," accessed June 8, 2016, http://www.history.com/topics/hurricane-katrina.

Chapter 23: Pray First
1. E.M. Bounds, as quoted in Mike Bickle, Growing in Prayer (Lake Mary, FL: Charisma House, 2014), 13.

www.ingramcontent.com/pod-product-compliance
Lightning Source LLC
Chambersburg PA
CBHW050538300426
44113CB00012B/2168